AF479287

Keisuke Fujiwara

Interior Elements for Space and Product Design

Frame Publishers

Chapter 1
×
Ambiguity

Chapter 2
×
Reawakened Form

Chapter 3
×
The Shape of Change

Chapter 4
×
The Pursuit of Possibilities

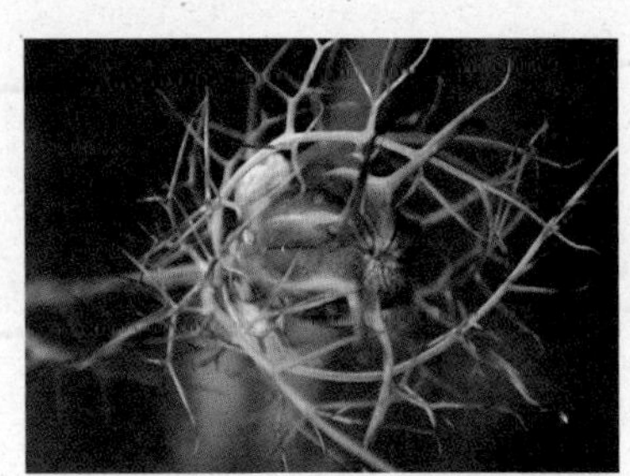

'Those in the field of *monozukuri* (the art of making things) lived and worked fervently through these times without stopping to acknowledge this change'

The wave of Westernisation that entered Japan in the latter half of the 19th century and increased its intensity in the 20th century, changed the lives of many. While it may lack a sense of reality for us, living in the present age, it imposed an unimaginably large change that can only be seen as we unravel the history of modern society. Some items we will be familiar with include the spread of technology and enhanced communication methods, the development of transportation and the means by which we travel, and the mass-production of home electronics.

Modern society may also be known as a period that has striven to overcome the inconveniences experienced in people's everyday lives. A great amount of wisdom came together in an effort to respond to people's wishes, tackling the countless problems encountered by society. As a result of hard work, life changed dramatically and innumerable people were liberated from the inconveniences encountered in their daily routine. Needless to say, the power of design played an enormous role in improving people's lives.

However, at some point, the wisdom employed in overcoming inconvenience came to be increasingly substituted as a tool for satisfying the desires of mankind. Those in the field of *monozukuri* (the art of making things) lived and worked fervently through these times without stopping to acknowledge this change. Many companies in our capitalistic society continued to overproduce, based on the pretext of making people's lives richer and more comfortable, and continued to pursue profit. They may have been wrongly convinced that meeting the demands of the users was the mission entrusted to design.

When I trace back their steps now, I cannot help but think that the tendencies to stimulate people's desires, to

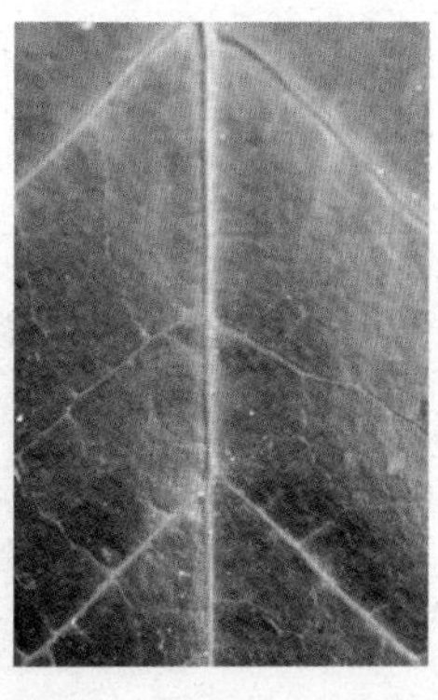

expand the market and to pursue rational economic efficiency were all too large. Moreover, this concept of market fundamentalism has become integrated into facets of our lives unaccustomed to it, like education, medicine, the cnvironment and even civic duty. This is what may have been implanted within the people, the disposition to think of all things in terms of money.

Modern ideas of the 20th century depicted society as a 'utopia' and proposed to solve all societal problems. When we look back on our world at the time, we can see that many people were led by the intentions of a society that prioritised the market economy. It may have been the case that, rather than building a society for people, it was in fact only those people that were convenient to society who became built into the social structure.

We now lead lives with little inconvenience, which may have consequently resulted in us leading lives with little opportunity for creativity. Creativity and compassion for others are important factors in our lives that help society function properly. Unfortunately, with the passing of time, we may also be leaving behind some such important things. Also, the lifestyles of people in developed nations – including Japan – have deviated little from such conditions laden with mankind's desires.

In the history of the Earth dating back 4.6 billion years, organisms came into existence, marking the creation of life, and after the passage of many long years, mankind was born. Bipedalism enabled human beings to support their developing physiology and, in turn, this enabled humans to acquire large brain capacities. Mankind, thus endowed with the highest intelligence of all animals, has since achieved striking progress.

Seen in the context of the long history of mankind, the modern age is but a mere dot of time. However, unfortunately, this period has given birth to a largely negative legacy in the earth's history. The various means of energy indispensable to mass consumption have continued to be used up to near exhaustion. The by-products created therein as well as the mechanisms devised by mankind for the creation of new energy sources have, depending on their use, become risks to the survival of the human race. People's everyday activities have heedlessly been led towards dangerous directions. Regardless, in our everyday lives, the age of glorified desire continues to reign with no significant change.

Nowadays, we often state that there are 'abnormal weather' conditions in terms of global warming, and various parts of the planet experience periods of unusually heavy rain, snow or high temperatures. Is it, however, a truly abnormal condition? While it may be the manifestation of an astrological cycle, perhaps nature is merely responding instinctively to all the environmental burdens unconsciously imposed by mankind. As long as the word 'abnormal weather' continues to be paraded about, I fear it shall not be possible to head in the direction of a sound environment.

In the early 20th century, before Westernisation gained momentum in Japan, the lives of the Japanese people were deeply connected to nature. One may even feel that what has been cultivated in days gone past, has since been buried by the wave of Westernisation. However, there are some things that have, slowly but surely, been inherited and passed on to the present age. In terms of architecture and interior design, they include the material and structure of buildings, the spatial structure of connecting the inside and outside of a building, and the means of framing a view of the out-

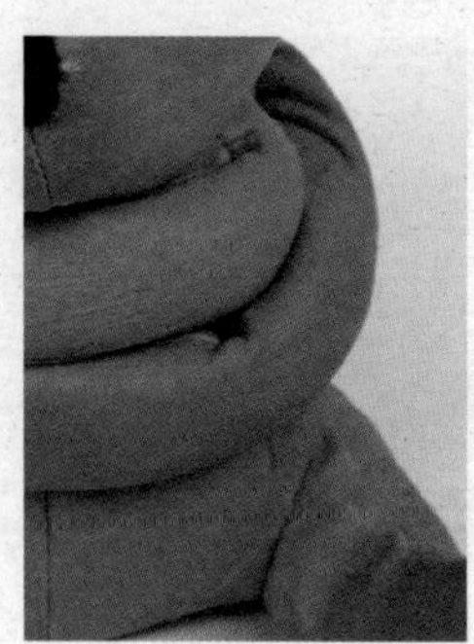

side landscape to be seen indoors. The biggest deciding factor in the creation of space has, in this way, been nature. The Japanese aesthetic sensibility, as represented by the word *kachoufugetsu* (the beauties of nature), has always adopted a vision of the essence of beauty in nature. In Japanese spaces, people's activities begin in an empty space. The *ba* (place) can be changed in accordance to the necessary uses through the tools brought into it. I believe that, even after the paradigm shift in our lifestyles after the early 20th century, some elements of this have still remained unchanged. In the Shitamachi (traditional shopping, entertainment and residential districts) of Tokyo where I grew up, a Hagoita-ichi (Battledore Festival) is held for the New Year at Asakusa Temple. A number of festivals are held from spring to summer and the delicate and beautiful form of the *mikoshi* (portable shrine) decorates the city as it is carried on the shoulders of the local people. When summer arrives, an Asagao-ichi (Morning Glory Fair) and Hozuki-ichi (Ground Cherry Fair) are also held. In the autumn, the Tori-no-ichi (Bird Day Festival) produces a lively atmosphere in the city. I have always experienced this culture throughout the year, close to my heart. As a young boy, I was always moved by the beauty within this culture and now it has somehow become an important aesthetic factor in my designs, acting as an index for my values.

I cannot imagine how many things may inspire people on a daily basis but – whether it a sky full of stars, the pure blue of the sky and sea, the enjoyment of live music, the exotic new worlds experienced through movies or books, the inspiring words imparted from a friend or the experience of art and design – there must be a multitude of experiences that remain etched within your heart. I have no doubt you have also experienced small sparks of inspiration in the simplest daily task as well.

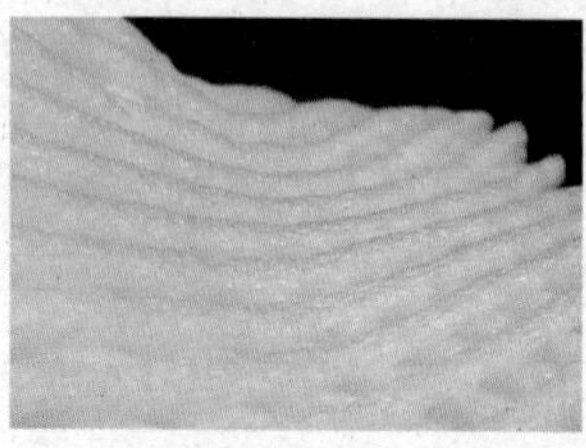

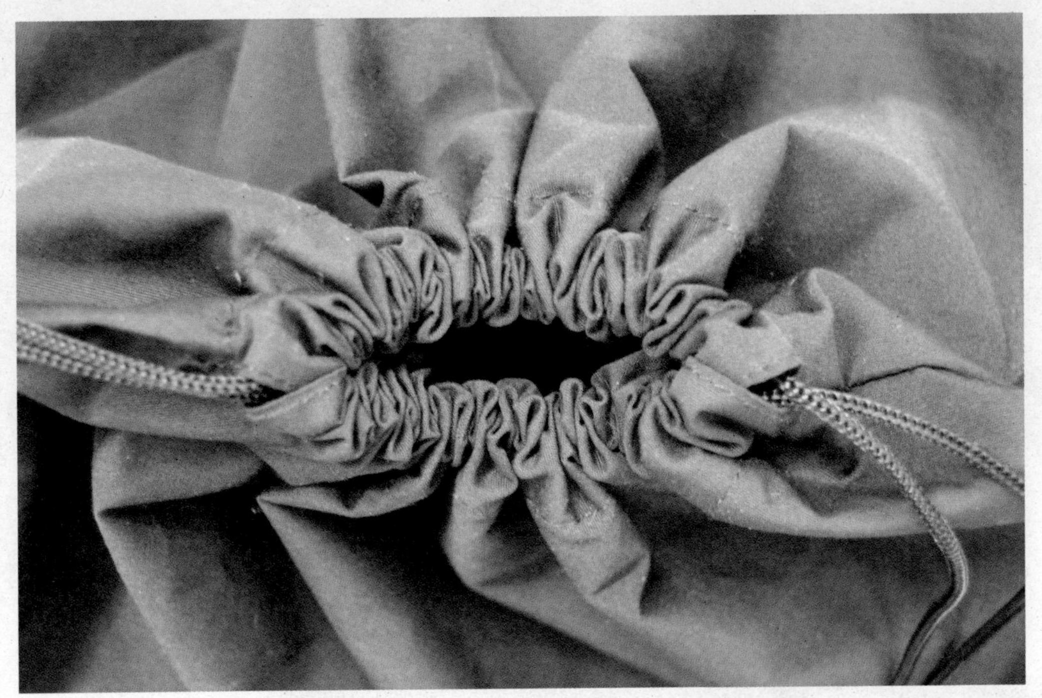

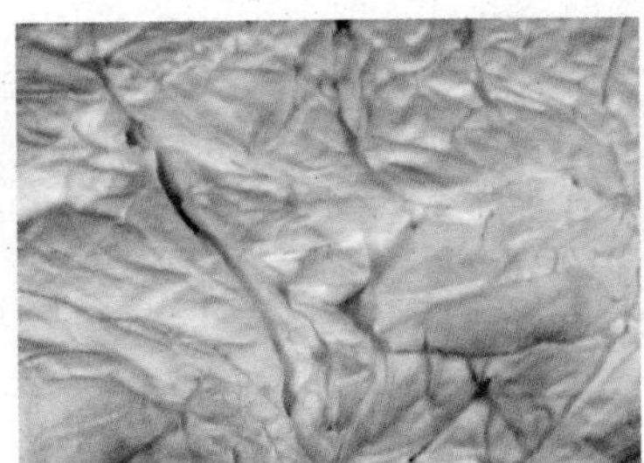

When I look back on the things that have inspired me, what is common to all of them is that they can all be interpreted as 'beautiful'. Perhaps this is because beauty reaches deep into our hearts and remains within, regardless of whether it has a physical form or not. When we see beauty, we feel uplifted. This uplifting feeling changes gradually over time to a quieter one; however, it is not erased from our memory but becomes a layer that enhances the richness of our hearts and is indispensable to shaping us as human beings. Although I have no scientific evidence of this, I believe that this feeling will revisit our memories throughout our lives and become the driving force that will lead our hearts in a healthier direction.

The yardstick by which we evaluate beauty is not uniform but comes in an infinite variety dependent on people. The sensation of 'beauty' leaves a vivid impression of the existence of an object or event, and leads to this being etched firmly in our minds. Whatever form it may come in, there is no doubt that it will fill our hearts with joy and become something that cannot be erased.

In my design work thus far, I have always thought of human activities, being mindful of creating and providing beauty that will reach deep into people's hearts. It has not been about meeting demands; instead, I have based it upon an ideal of providing something that can be likened to nutrients poured into the empty bowls within our bodies, waiting to be filled. What I have pursued are things that are indispensable – in other words, beauty that is necessary for human beings.

This book is not centred on methodologies or means for beautifying the *ba* (places) of human activity. Instead I will be introducing the thought processes and ideas on human activity and the creation of *ba* that I always keep in mind when designing. I have roughly divided these into four elements and will introduce what I have practiced in design through examples of actual projects.

The first of these elements is 'Ambiguity'. While it is hard to grasp and express in words, this indicates the beauty felt by our senses, resounding deep within our hearts. The second is 'Reawakened Form'. This is the rediscovery of beauty, focusing on the things that lie hidden within our daily lives. It also includes things that we may have left behind in the passage of time, as well as things that we hope to foster within us with utmost care. The third is 'The Shape of Change', describing things that instantaneously or gradually change. I believe that beauty lies hidden in the transience and affection we feel for things that change. The fourth is 'The Pursuit of Possibilities'. I believe that the challenge and acts of experimentation and validation lead to beauty and further to the sublimation of beauty. Apart from this, I will describe how I was challenged by each project, what I pondered and puzzled over, and what I did to overcome the problems I encountered, in a chronological order for each project. 'Beautiful interior design' is what I strive for.

I would be delighted if, after reading this book, you begin to notice the many charms that lie hidden within your everyday lives which may elicit small changes in your heart. It would further be my utmost pleasure if you could develop even the slightest interest in the world of interior design and if this book could provide for you a little power to carry on with your daily life. ×

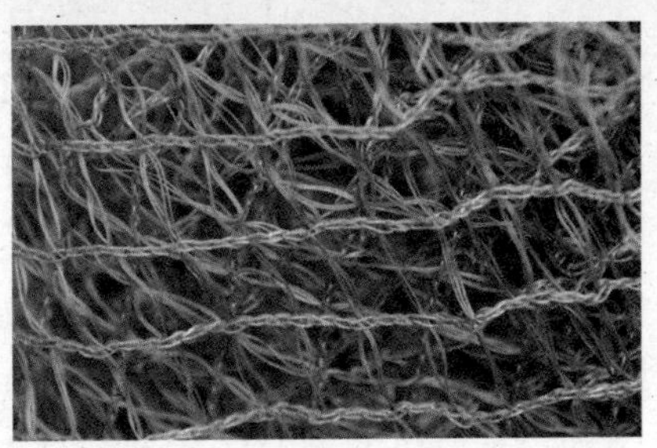

Supporting people's everyday activities – this is what I have striven to accomplish through my work in interior design. My mentor, the designer Shigeru Uchida, has stated in his book, *A History of Design in Postwar Japan*, that design is 'to think about how human beings can live soundly upon Earth, to give concrete form and to create the mechanisms for achieving this idea'. He has further stated that 'design can be called an act to connect all elements surrounding human beings, including society and nature and to endow practicality to society'. In this regard, interior design is not only about space, nor is it only about products like furniture. What is important is to raise topics questioning what mankind is or what it means to live, to secure a fluid balance composed of interior elements and to constantly ponder the relationship between body and space.

Interior elements indicate the various factors that compose space. To design interior elements means to contemplate the creation of foundations spanning the realm of interior design. This includes elements that divide space, such as floors, walls and ceilings, as well as things set in space, such as chairs, tables, shelves and lights. They further include sound, light and smell, invisible to the naked eye. The shapes, sizes, colours, textures and other various factors composing such elements largely contribute to the relationships involved in interior design. Interior design is therefore not an extraordinary idea but a concept that is always close to us. One of its roles includes the visualisation of shared sensibilities that we may only have vague conceptions of. It is the creation of culture through materialisation, supporting people's happiness not only from a materialistic perspective but a psychological one as well. ×

Chapter 1
×
Ambiguity

Pleats Please Issey Miyake

Taipei Miramar

In this shop, my goal was not to produce an interior design emphasising the unique qualities of the brand but to create what may be called a 'clothing plaza' decorated with clothes. The starting point for the spatial design was the image of the Pleats Please Issey Miyake clothing waving gently in a plaza where a gentle breeze and delicate scent graces the skin of the customers.

I opened up the area facing the corridor with the idea of fashioning it into a *ba* (place) that could be walked by casually without drawing too much attention from passers-by. The space has circular elements scattered throughout: the three pillars with symbolic presence that simultaneously partition each *ba* ambiguously, the hanger pipes attached to these pillars, the rotating display shelves and the shelves built into the wall, as well as the tables and the sofas make up the furniture in this space. These can be approached from various directions and have been designed for ease of passage through the space and for creating a sense of openness. Each circular element is assembled in ten different scales, each fulfilling its function with regard to their mutual balance.

The gradient film covering the columns and wall, changing in colour from white to light blue, has been adopted in multiple Pleats Please Issey Miyake shops throughout Japan. This sheet was first created in order to fashion a space where one could experience the slight tinge of colour that remains in the heart. What I mean by this is that, when you are in the space looking at the products, you take in your surroundings as being just white; however, I hope that a subtle memory of colour accompanies you upon leaving the space. This sheet was printed on a large-format inkjet printer in a gradient colour and applied on the white interior fixtures.

The ability to exchange data between Japan and Taiwan using only the internet and to provide building materials unique to the brand without shipping anything may be a distinct characteristic of this modern age. When building materials are shipped across the sea, many problems unique to this age are encountered, such as the consumption of energy and appropriate costs, as well as time efficiency. I think of my interior designs for Pleats Please Issey Miyake as one method for solving such issues. Thinking of the problems engendered by society from various angles and continuing to search for the best solutions to them is one of the most indispensable roles of interior design. ×

Where **Taipei, Taiwan**
When **October 2004**
Project type **Boutique**
Photographer **Satoshi Asakawa**

PLEATS
PLEASE

'The starting point imagined the clothing waving in a gentle breeze'

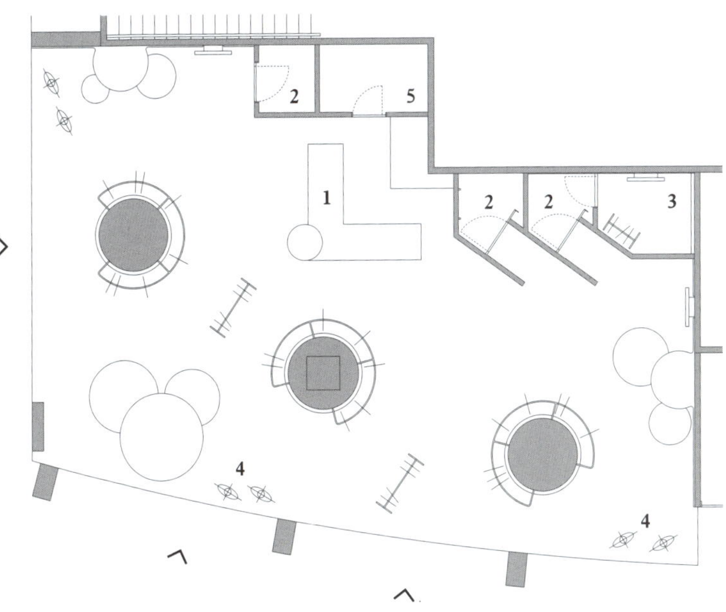

Floor Plan

1. Counter
2. Changing room
3. VIP changing room
4. Window display
5. Stockroom

'I hope that a subtle memory of colour accompanies you upon leaving the space'

Gradation film studies.

PLEATS
PLEASE
ISSEY MIYAKE

Pleats Please Issey Miyake

Kaohsiung President

This shop was opened in a department store in Kaohsiung, located on the southern tip of Taiwan. It was important for this interior, neighbouring the escalator hall, to welcome people from all directions. Therefore, it was necessary to create a space with an unobstructed view, having no set orientation as to the front or back of the store. I thus designed the space considering the perspective of those going up and down the adjacent escalators, and understanding the space itself from various angles.

Products of the Pleats Please range are made of polyester formed into pleats. This creates layers in the polyester. The spatial design adopted the keyword 'layers' as its theme, derived from the characteristics of the products.

The fitting room, stock room, shelves and counters were designed to retain their function while appearing like large, rectangular volumes placed in the space. Adding height to these volumes, I tried to create a form in which these volumes were layered upon one another. My idea was to create an open feel and an experience of a separate world found by stepping just one foot into the store. Additionally, the focus on a unique lighting design – different from the neighbouring shops – has perhaps given rise to the adequate sense of tension within the quiet of the space. ×

Where **Kaohsiung, Taiwan**
When **June 2008**
Project type **Boutique**
Photographer **Satoshi Asakawa**

Display shelf and pillar finished by gradation film.

PLEATS
PLEASE
ISSEY MIYAKE

PLEATS
PLEASE

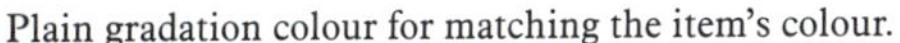

Plain gradation colour for matching the item's colour.

Displaying pale coloured clothing in front of the gradation coloured wall.

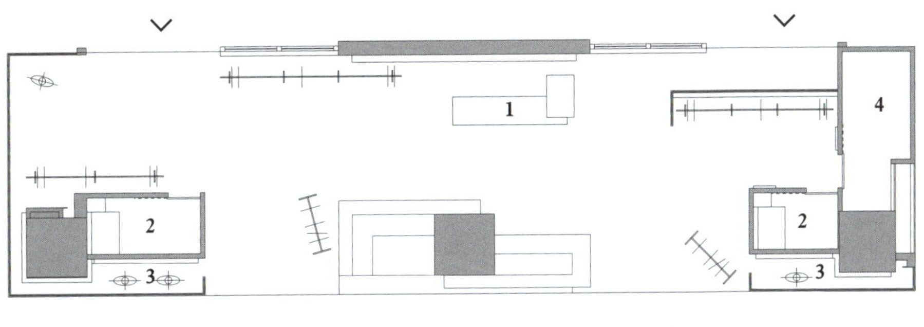

Floor Plan

1. Counter
2. Changing room
3. Window display
4. Stockroom

'I layered large, rectangular volumes upon one another'

Pleats Please Issey Miyake

Kokura Isetan

This shop is located in one of the most prominent department stores in Kyushu. It was a space that was far from spacious, surrounded by walls on three sides. A column also stood in the centre of the space and, with the limited area inside the shop, this structural element had much potential to become a negative element in the space.

Here, I decided to incorporate a voluminous shelf into the central column to heighten the presence of the column, such that it would become the element governing the impression of the space. I installed indirect lighting on the underside of the shelf to produce a lighter sense of space and I also consciously worked to create an interior that would leave a lingering impression. The functions of hanger pipes were located along the surrounding walls in such a way as to minimise their presence as much as possible.

Angles – neither perpendicular nor parallel to the ground – were used here and there. This was done to help draw customers into the space and aid their view of the products, as well as to create rhythm and intonation in the space.

The gradations used on the walls were not created in a single direction; instead, patterns with vertical and horizontal movements were adopted. This produced a slightly aggressive impression for the space. ×

Where **Fukuoka, Japan**
When **February 2004**
Project type **Boutique**
Photographer **Kanta Ushio**

PLEATS
PLEASE
ISSEY MIYAKE

PLEATS
PLEASE
ISSEY MIYAKE

'I used angles to create rhythm and intonation in the space'

5 pm in the Summer

In designing this titanium chair, my greatest efforts went into creating a sharp and elegant figure from the back. Titanium is strong, light, corrosion- and heat-resistant and is used in a variety of fields. With a colour composition that could only be expressed through anodisation, the distinctive features of this chair include its colour and production process. As the title suggests as well, it was based on the image of a summer sunset.

The anodisation process for the titanium used in this product results in the oxidation of the material's surface. In other words, electricity is applied to the material to force it to rust, thereby creating an oxide film through a chemical process. This oxide film has a transparent membrane with a high index of refraction and assumes the role of a prism, thus refracting light. The refraction index also changes based on the thickness of the oxide film and, due to the interference between light waves, it goes on to create a dyed appearance in the product.

The first step in the production process of this chair entailed a preliminary treatment to remove any unnecessary fingerprints or other trace elements left on the titanium surface from the processing work. After the surface was cleaned, the material was anodised by soaking in electrolytic solution. Pulling the chair out of the electrolytic solution while altering the voltage applied created changes in the thickness of the oxide film through the voltage difference. This, in turn, created the differences in colouring.

First realised in 2001, five kinds of chair and two tables were created as a part of this anodised titanium series by 2007, amounting to one piece produced per year. That year, I held an exhibition during the Milan Salone in Italy where these products were first presented. This then led to the opportunity to present my works at Design Miami in December 2007, followed by an invitation to present at the International Design Biennale in Kortrijk held the following year in 2008.

Were the dining chair, the origin of this very chair, to be considered an adaptive element blending into its surroundings, then this titanium chair would be one that exerts its own presence in the space. If we view a chair in relation to the *ba* (place) it is in, it is clear that these chairs identify on opposite sides of the spectrum. ×

When **2001–2007**
Project type **Seating**
Photographer **Satoshi Asakawa**

Initial sketch for the chair design, emphasising its distinctive colours.

'With its distinctive colours, I based this chair on the image of a summer sunset'

'I consider this chair as an adaptive element, blending into its surroundings'

'The colour composition is expressed through a process of titanium anodisation'

The process of colour coating by anodisation.

Reflection Sofa

Most sofas are big, heavy and stable. While this is one of the charms of a sofa, I sometimes wonder if it could have a slightly lighter impression, considering the balance between the space and sofa and the time spent therein.

The design shown detailed here is extremely simple with regard to its form. The overall form has a voluminous feel that is very similar to that of a cube. The main difference is that the legs were cut into arcs to prevent it from assuming a heaviness. I attempted to emphasise a lightweight impression by keeping the contact between the chair and floor to a bare minimum.

The chair itself is made of fibre-reinforced plastic. Thus, the inside of this sofa (the underside) is hollow. I painted the interior (underside) with neon paint. This, in turn, reflected colour onto the floor, emitting a faint, colourful glow around the sofa. This was an important factor in further establishing its look of lightness.

This strong focus on the inside (underside) producing a modest look of elegance, rather than a showy appearance, may be something that Japanese *monozukuri* has always regarded with importance and care. While the inside (underside) expression employed here cannot, by any means, be considered a successor to what has been engendered in the Japanese cultural background, it is a design theme that I would like to continue to explore as a new approach to design. ×

When **2013**
Project type **Seating**
Photographer **Satoshi Asakawa**

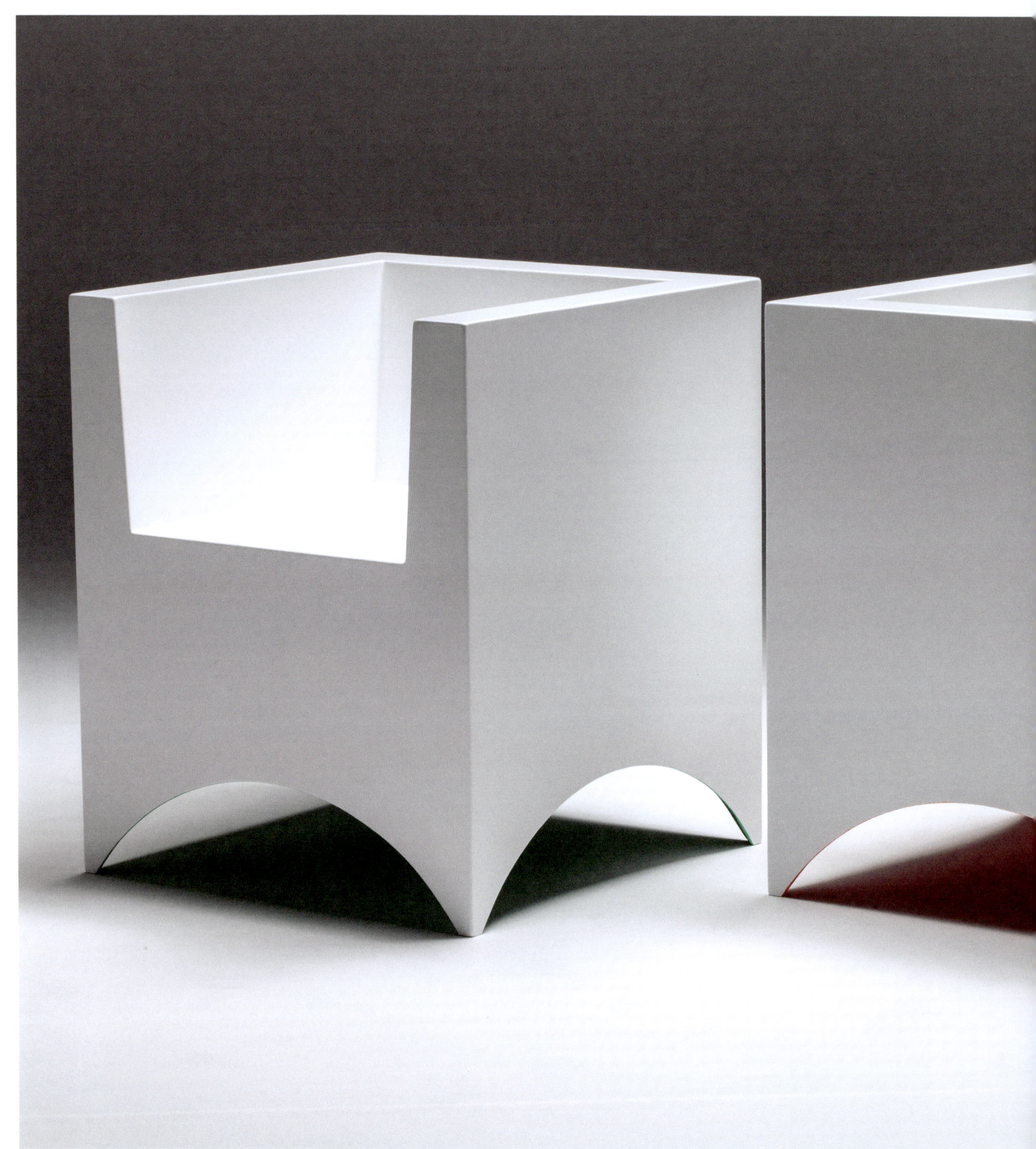

'My intended design here was extremely simple with regard to its form'

The chairs were designed to create a coloured reflection on the floor.

Pleats Please Issey Miyake

Taipei 101

The space allotted to this Pleats Please Issey Miyake store faces a dynamic circular atrium. One of the unique features of this space is its 4-m-high ceiling. The first design solution I came up with here was to divide the space horizontally in two, and allocate different uses to the top and bottom spaces. The top layer was created to present the overall impression of the space, while the bottom layer was equipped with the functions of a shop.

Polarised acrylic panels embedded with 10 layers of graphics were used to produce lightness and movement in the upper layer of the space. The cool colours of the wall follow human movement, undergoing subtle changes throughout the space. This design was inspired by the cover of a book that I had come across long ago while travelling through Europe, which I had made note of to use someday as an interior design element.

The bottom layer, on the other hand was covered in square bars emphasising the horizontal plane. These bars form a corrugated pattern, becoming hanger pipes for displaying products in one instance, or shelves for placing knick-knacks in another, then becoming counters for working and waiting on customers and providing indirect lighting for the space. In this way, these bars change form and exist in close relation to the space, providing the necessary functions of the shop.

The targeted market is global, as international brands are found in a variety of countries and regions throughout the world. In order to pursue a certain image, most brands create manuals for their spatial designs. However, I believe that rather than designs based on manuals, spatial designs for international brands require fluidity to flexibly respond to the conditions given by the individual country or region they are in.

I do not know how many brands actually practice this concept, but I believe the true beauty of interior design lies in pursuing the unlimited possibilities of spatial design with each space, while preserving consistency in the brand. I reaffirmed the true joys of pursuing such design in working on this shop. Such an opportunity is not possible without the strong philosophy of the client and brand, as well as the power of the product. In this sense, Pleats Please Issey Miyake can be considered a rare brand with products that embody excitement and a strong philosophy. ×

Where **Taipei, Taiwan**
When **April 2004**
Project type **Boutique**
Photographer **Satoshi Asakawa**

'This design was inspired by the cover of a book that I had come across long ago while travelling through Europe'

PLEATS
PLEASE
ISSEY MIYAKE

'I believe true beauty of interior design lies in pursuing the unlimited possibilities of spatial design while preserving consistency in the brand'

Floor Plan

1. Counter
2. Changing room
3. Window display
4. Stockroom

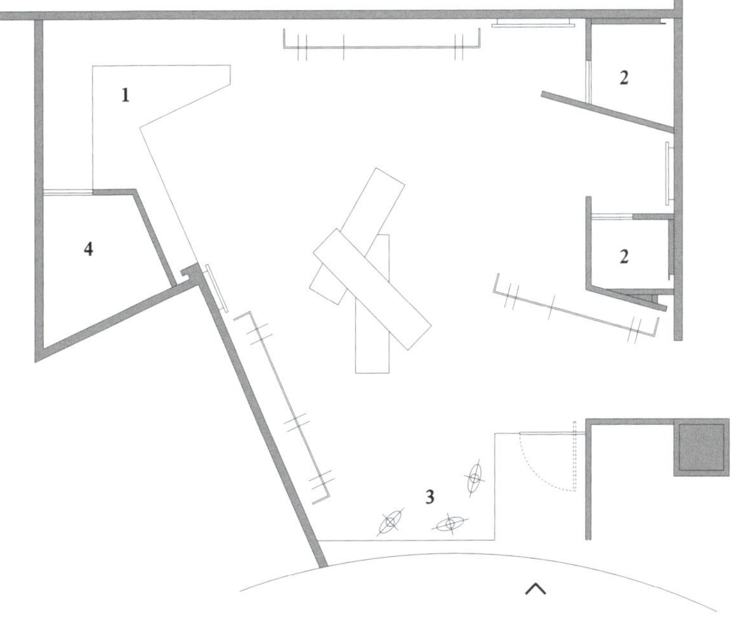

Colour-Changing Shelf

These are designs for cupboards affixed to the wall. Lenticular sheets are applied to the surfaces of the hinged doors of these shelves. The patterns on this lenticular sheet begin to move upon the opening and closing of the doors. I have designed with this material a few times already, but the idea behind these designs was the relationship between the fixed lenticular sheet and our movements.

One of my goals in this design was to create a relationship in which the lenticular sheet would be actively moved. As the sheets were applied to cabinet doors, dynamic changes could be observed. There are two variations to this design: one in which the full surface changes dynamically in rainbow colours, and the other in which a small grid format changes subtly from cool to warm colours.

My preoccupation here was with surface design; however, I was also conscious of two points on the shelf itself. The first was about the hinges. Metal hinges are typically used in such designs but, because I did not want superfluous elements to be seen when the doors opened, I decided to use canvas for the hinges. There is a magnetic catch embedded in the main frame of the shelf. While the form is neatly streamlined without any unnecessary elements, there remains the secure, comforting feeling of clicking the cabinet door closed. ×

When **2002**
Project type **Cupboard**
Photographer **Satoshi Asakawa**

The surface colour of the lenticular sheet on the door changes dynamically by opening.

Pleats Please Issey Miyake

Galeries Lafayette Paris

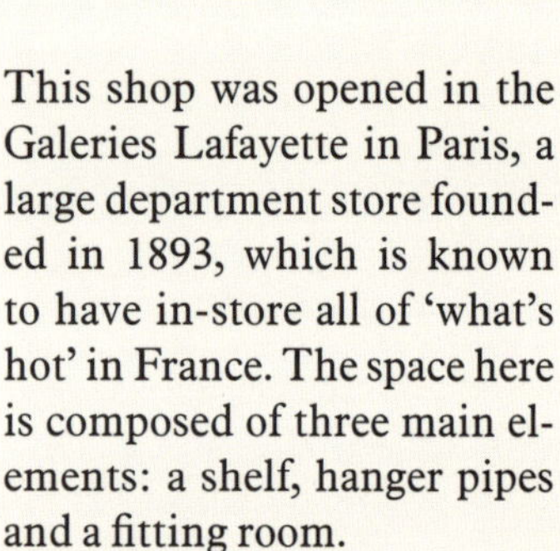

This shop was opened in the Galeries Lafayette in Paris, a large department store founded in 1893, which is known to have in-store all of 'what's hot' in France. The space here is composed of three main elements: a shelf, hanger pipes and a fitting room.

The shelf, incorporated into the work counter, provides a space for waiting on customers, as well as displaying products. Furthermore, one of its goals is to be a symbolic, sculptural element that serves to preserve the image of the space in the minds of its visitors. The elegantly curving silhouette of the hanger pipes is a form that I devised in order to foster an understanding of the light and delicate quality of Pleats Please Issey Miyake products. Additionally, I used warm and cool colours in the interiors of the two fitting rooms to provide a small sense of surprise. This is seen in the pale colour emitted on the ceiling outside the fitting room.

This department store has been designated as a historical building in France, so it may already be familiar to many people. The dome-shaped, Neo-Byzantine style stained glass creates an overpowering space. The creation of a store in such a building where the new and the old coincide was a rare experience, hard to come across in Japan. ×

Where **Paris, France**
When **March 2002**
Project type **Boutique**
Photographer **Gitty Darugar**

'I envisioned the shelf to be a symbolic, sculptural element'

PLEATS
PLEASE
ISSEY MIYAKE

Pleats Please Issey Miyake

Seoul Galleria

This was the first Pleats Please Issey Miyake shop established in Korea. Its location was in the Seoul Galleria shopping plaza's fashion hall. Here, lenticular sheets – the main material used for the brand's development at the time – were used dynamically rather than as an accent, covering three sides of the upper space.

Indirect lighting was fit into this three-sided enclosure to sweep away the heavy appearance. As it would also be a place for displaying products, I further established a lighting scheme that enabled illumination to reach the products. One of the hanger racks, fixed to the wall, takes on a form that stretches away from the wall. The products displayed here act as elements that gently block the view from the counter. A highly mobile display shelf is set in the middle of the space, so that the changes in the shop can be enjoyed not just by the customers but by the staff as well.

The lenticular sheets were available in Korea at the time. However, although the use of local materials would normally be preferred, because instability in the precision of producing the material still remained an issue in Japan at the time, I decided to refrain from procuring it on-site. The project thus progressed by removing these issues one by one, with production in Japan and subsequent shipping to Korea. ×

Where **Seoul, Korea**
When **September 2002**
Project type **Boutique**
Photographer **Kim Kwang Ook**

PLEATS
PLEASE
ISSEY MIYAKE

Pleats Please Issey Miyake

Shinjuku Isetan

This branch was opened in one of the leading department stores in Japan. The design of fixtures in this space was based on the concept of making them easily moveable by a store staff member. Each piece was thus not fixed in place but instead was made mobile, light, compact and stable.

In the moveable hanger pipes, the appearance of mobility was pursued along with its physical mobility. The pipe texture, colour and overall finish were determined through countless samples, experimentation and validation, checking the material's balance in relation to the product and the space as well as its durability. I also incorporated symbolic characteristics of buoyancy and mobility through elements like the details of the pipe joints and the caster-shaped rubber rings on the bottom of the legs.

The shelf frames also employed the material used in the hanger rack. The display area on the shelf was made of 25-mm transparent acrylic boards covered with view-control film, which appears either transparent or frosted based on the angle of view. Here, it appears transparent from afar, creating the impression of floating, and frosted up-close. Another characteristic is that it helps light from the ceiling reach below the shelf. ×

Where **Tokyo, Japan**
When **February 2002**
Project type **Boutique**
Photographer **Satoshi Asakawa**

PLEATS
PLEASE

Spool Chair

This is a chair fashioned on the concept of spools of thread. The chair was exhibited at Design Miami, a design event held in Miami in December of 2007. I happened to visit a shop in my neighborhood that sold fabrics and sewing materials and fell in love with the beauty of the rich colours of the fabrics covering the walls. I couldn't resist buying a few to take home and, after putting some thought into what I could do with them, they became the inspiration for this design. The idea materialised as I began winding a few strands of thread around a stick. The design progressed from here, until I had wrapped an entire chair in thread.

I decided that, in this project, there was no need to create a new form for this design and thought it most appropriate to use a chair that everybody knows – hence, the Thonet Chair No. 14 was the one selected to be entwined in thread. Yet another deciding factor for using this chair was its woven cane seat. Becoming aware of the considerable amount of time and work that would be necessary to completely cover the chair in thread, further heightened my eagerness to take on the challenge. I then felt with certainty that it would surely succeed in expressing the beauty of the colour composition made from wrapped threads as well as the appeal of *monozukuri* (the art of making things) infused with the lingering reverberations of handicrafts. Thus began my days of earnest engagement with utmost respect for this chair enveloped in history.

At the outset, I decided on a colour composition and guidelines for the direction of my design. I then chose 12 ultra-thin nylon threads and began to wrap the threads around the chair, trusting my senses. The chair composed of warm colours was named 'Fire', while the one in cool colours was entitled 'Water'. The state of the chairs in progress was entitled 'Water Process'. Although not pictured in the photos here, there is also a chair entitled 'Ground', based on the image of the earth and composed of earth colours. To wrap one of the chairs, approximately 12 km of thread is required.

My idea here was not to simply pursue rationality or uniformity in *monozukuri* but to consciously incorporate elements considered unnecessary for mass production, like the senses, vestiges of things and irrationality. I believe that within this, we encounter a great many wonders, such as the traces of the hand, which have been excluded in mass-produced items. This project helped refresh my notion that hints for design lie in things familiar to us and that the important thing is how to grasp these without losing sight of them. ×

When **2007**
Project type **Seating**
Photographer **Satoshi Asakawa**

Fire (left) and Water (right).

'Expressing the beauty of a colour composition as well as the appeal of *monozukuri* (the art of making things)'

'The concept materialised as I began winding strands of thread around a stick'

Traditional handicrafts were at the heart of the production process.

Flowers for 365 Days

This is a single-flower vase designed with the names of birth flowers for each of the 365 days of the year were spelled out to form a spiralling chain of letters. My idea was to form this chain of letters into a silhouette of a vase.

The technology used for this process was laser marking. In this procedure, the general physical effects of melting, burning, peeling, oxidising, scraping and discolouring the surface of objects by irradiating them with a laser light. Data is converted to an exclusive file format and laser rays are applied based on this data. As laser beams are applied from two directions, cracks appear where the two beams coincide, creating a two- or three-dimensional engraving on the inside of a crystal glass block.

However, this vase was made from a transparent acrylic block and not glass. Laser beams with a high peak-to-peak value were concentrated inside this block to create cracks. The components in the acrylic reacted like glass to create cracks that changed to a white colour. The objects engraved by this laser marking were letters of the alphabet formed by this collective accumulation of cracks. I had more and more opportunities to talk to manufacturers who could provide this technology, some of whom kindly visited me from abroad. However, I was faced with many new problems that I had yet to solve, such as the detailed nature of the design, the processable block size and the need to create a hole for the flower. Thus, it took a number of years to actually realise the design.

What I pondered over most in this design was how to form the hole in this single-flower vase. I made countless attempts through trial-and-error before finally arriving at this design. Considering the balance between the silhouette and the size of the hole, I knew I could not create a hole that was too big. Even if I were able to create a large hole, it would not be able to penetrate through the vase, which brought up another problem of being unable to polish the inside surface. Acrylic surfaces that cannot be polished become white, and this white surface would then stand out. As this would result in a deviation from my concept of not drawing attention to the hole, I had to readdress this issue of possible hole diameters and depths with manufacturers time and again until a solution was found and the vase took its final form. ×

When **2007**
Project type **Vase**
Photographer **Satoshi Asakawa / Nacasa & Partners**

'My idea was to have a spiralling chain of flower names, one for every day of the year'

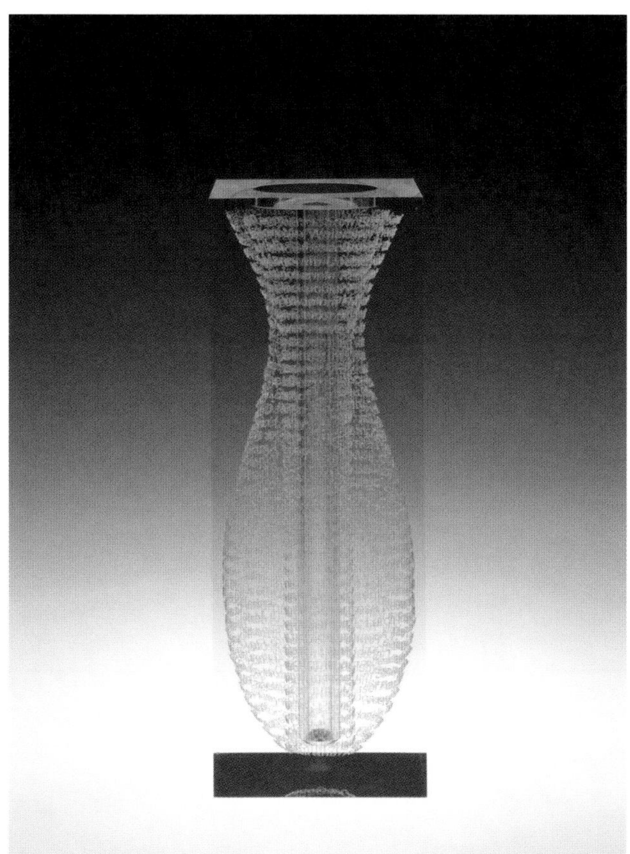

The names of birth flowers for each of the 365 days of the year were spelled out to form a spiral chain of letters.

The word 'design' has come to penetrate our everyday lives. With the word 'interior design', more than a few people may imagine colours and materials for designing an interior space, as well as the selection of such products. These things are, of course, indispensable to design. However, in reality, design does not stop at such a narrow definition; instead, it may not be an exaggeration to state that it encompasses the much wider meaning of 'thinking about the future that human beings will be living in'.

The activities involved in living vary largely amongst different races, cultures and times. However, the most basic activities of humankind – such as eating, resting and sleeping – stay constant. In other words, the basis of human life has not changed over the years.

The leading role in life is played by people. In other words, all of Earth's people assume the role of the protagonist. Providing a moving experience for such people, possible only through interior design, and touching the hearts of each and every one of them is, I believe, one of the most important tasks for those working in the field of design.

Thus far, in all of my interior design work, I have always considered how beautifully an individual's presence could be reflected in a space. What I mean by this is, for instance, time spent with family full of smiles around a dining table, an environment for spending time with friends and opening our hearts to one another, or the air of anticipation felt when stepping one foot into the finest spaces in which we can focus our minds – reviewing such wholesome activities of human beings will eventually result in extracting the beauty of design, perhaps because it is there that the most basic beauty of our lives as human beings could be found. I believe that beauty will always exist within designs born from respecting and taking a true look at human activities. ×

Chapter 2 × Reawakened Form

Sora

When I begin an interior design job, I often decide to leave the existing architectural framework or the minimum facilities untouched. So, when I saw the herringbone tiles on the floor in this space, I knew it was a legacy that I had to leave intact for the future. This came to have a huge influence on the later progress of the design and, especially in the selection of materials, it was this herringbone tile-look that guided the selection of the remaining materials and tone.

When the hair-salon firm Sora decided to open a third branch on Gakugei University campus, my highest priority was to create something that would act as an axis for the spatial design, so I tried to connect the attractive elements of the first and second stores. This was a task akin to fitting in the pieces of a puzzle.

A pool of water greets customers at the entrance. Each droplet of water that drips down into the pool creates a ripple accompanied by light and a faint sound. This was designed with the hope of making people feel more at ease. The overall lighting scheme was decided so as not to interfere with the work of hairdressing or discerning the highlights in hair colouring. In the shampoo area, equipped with fully reclining seats, I decided against installing ceiling lights, so as to avoid glare and create soft indirect light that would gently envelop the body.

Additionally, in order to further connect 'space, time and people', I kept the existing 20-year-old flooring and glass sashes used in this space almost fully intact. My hopes were to pass down this 'lamination of time' developed over the ages into the future. The louver partitions made of a seemingly random composition of 12 different kinds of wood materials were organised to form a somewhat recognisable alphabet – but only when viewed in the mirror would visitors see that it spelt the salon's name 'Sora'. The hair-styling mirrors placed before each seat were constructed in reference to the size of the *Mona Lisa* painting by Leonardo da Vinci.

Furthermore, the contrast of dark and light toned wood materials used in the first and second stores came together as one in this third store, through the use and effect of the 12 different wood tones. The colours of these varying wood tones change as powerfully as the morning sun and are based on the image of the *sora* (sky), providing comfort as gently as the setting sun and becoming the symbolic element for this salon. ×

Where **Tokyo, Japan**
When **January 2009**
Project type **Salon**
Photographer **Satoshi Asakawa**

An eye-catching water sculpture is positioned near the entrance.

'I often decide to leave the existing architectural frame-work intact, as a legacy for the future'

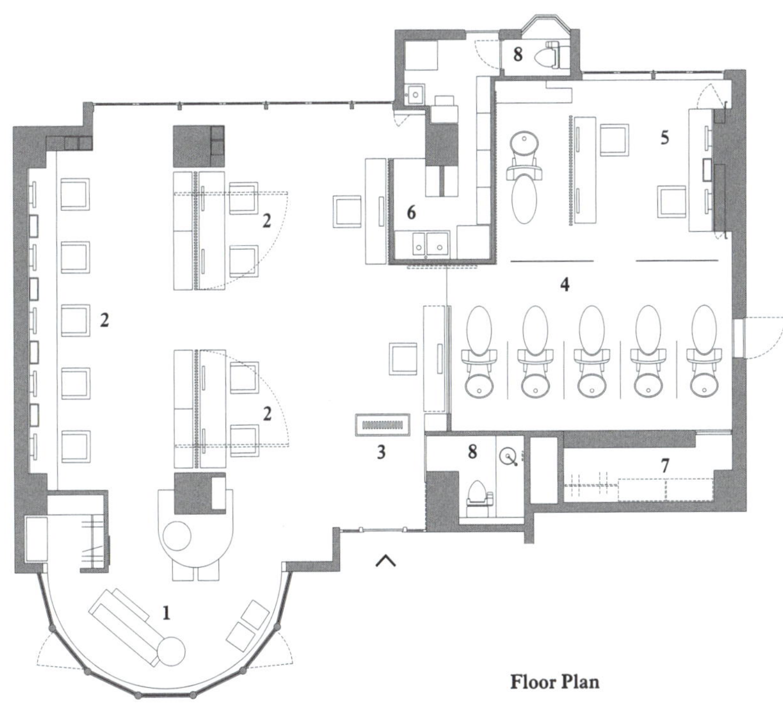

Floor Plan

1. Reception
2. Styling area
3. Water sculpture
4. Shampoo area
5. Styling room
6. Staff room
7. Stockroom
8. Toilet

‘I chose the colours of the varying wood tones as a symbolic element for this salon’

The partition with gradation colour using several wood tones.

The letters 'SORA' are incorporated into the partition by the use of several timber colours.

Moon Chair

Here, I introduce a chair that I designed for a television series. This project had a more transitory feel compared to my usual designs because it was meant for a fictional world. During the early stages of the process, instead of the simple task of purely designing a chair, I set forth on this task as though I were fashioning an actor for a scene.

All my energy went into designing this chair, as it would appear in the final episode of the TV series, and the design concept was a critical point in the show. The momentum of everyone involved in the TV series came together in the design and production of this chair. In the episode, this chair appears at the climax of the story when the protagonist, who had experienced betrayal and had resigned from presidency, designs this chair as a means of returning to his roots. In a design competition, he proposes this linking chair under the concept that 'chairs are meant to be for people'.

Once I received the script for this final episode, I drew sketch upon sketch while reading the script to create the right image. As there were scenes in which the actors would carry around the chair, I considered ease of holding and carrying. Thus, while structural strength would slightly decrease because of this, I decided to make the chair legs slimmer than in my usual designs. It was a fresh new experience for me to build on my imagination of the scene while simultaneously conceptualising the chair's form.

The chair, appearing in the final episode of this drama, also had to be capable of linking together. I thus decided that the silhouette of the five chairs placed side by side should create the form of a mountain. And, in order to symbolically express the drama's keyword, 'moon', I cut a moon-shaped slit into one of the backrests. It was a truly valuable experience for me to design based on the completely new approach of reading a script and imagining the scenes of a show.

All the projects I had designed before, had been within the realm of the non-fictional world. In this project, I imagined the hidden world of the story and designed its fictional world. While it required work from a perspective different to my usual designs, there were some commonalities in the basic process of realising something that I had designed. Designing furniture requires imagining people's behaviours and activities, and it is this imagination that leads to solidifying the critical framework for design. ×

When **2010**
Project type **Seating**
Photographer **Satoshi Asakawa**

Exhibition of New Textile Works by Kawashima Textile Manufacturers #1

The founding of the traditional textile company in Japan, Kawashima Textile Manufacturers, dates far back to the year 1843 (Tenpo 14). The firm is known for the production of the most quintessential industrial art pieces, such as festival curtains for the Gion Festival and mosquito nets, as well as the manufacturing of traditional obi sashes.

In the exhibition hall, I tried to create a world of darkness, completely removed from the white world of the first floor. For this, I had some large spools of thread, 10 km in length and in over 500 different colours, brought over from a manufacturer in Kyoto. This not only functioned as the spatial design symbol but also the symbol for textile cloth, as well as the company, and was thus placed at the centre of the exhibition. This scene of threads strung between the ceiling and floor like bowstrings was inspired by what I had seen at the manufacturer's factory in Kyoto.

I wanted people to see this simple beauty, so I adopted it as a symbol in the spatial composition. My idea was that through the dialogue of seeing and the dialogue of feeling through experience, the shared perception of beauty would deepen connections between people.

Lastly, the new products and their descriptions were hung from the ceiling and placed around the perimeter of the space to demonstrate the company's attitude of continuously challenging various endeavours, rather than in a spatial design for viewing each textile one by one. ×

Where **Tokyo, Japan**
When **December 2001**
Project type **Exhibition**
Photographer **Satoshi Asakawa**

In the installation, threads were strung between the ceiling and the floor.

'I wanted people to see the simple beauty, so I adopted it as a symbol in the spatial composition'

feel good
KAWASHIMA
E-grass
KAWASHIMA
ポリプロピレン染色
リサイクル

KAWASHIMA
FAB-ACE

Marronnier Gate

This is the design for a commercial centre in Tokyo's Ginza district, which has long valued its *machiaruki* (walk around the district). The joy of walking around Ginza has been passed on down through the generations. One of the reasons for this may be the ease of walking in this area. Its main streets and alleyways intersect to create moments of liveliness and quiet that reinforce one another to connect the city to its people, the shops to the people and people to one another. This appeal of a city at human scale, in which we can encounter new discoveries while out walking, is one of the characteristics of Ginza that has continued on to this day – a valuable inheritance to pass on to the future.

For this project, I focused on an understanding of a commercial facility, stretching from the basement to the twelth floor as stratified layers of shopping streets, with the goal of recreating the joys of *machiaruki* in a vertical fashion. What was important here was not to isolate the facility as a separate entity, but to bring the characteristics cultured by the Ginza district into its interior environment. My goal was to highlight the tenants' most attractive qualities by creating a non-uniform space rich in variation while also modest in character. The changes and discoveries found with each movement through the space emulate the characteristics of Ginza's *machiaruki* in a stratified, modern spatial design.

Each floor was assigned one of five keywords: root, trunk, branch, leaf or flower. This was used as both the material for developing the spatial design, as well as a decision-making factor in the design. With a need to create varying expressions from the basement to the top floor, the system mixed together a myriad of ingredients, rare to find in a facility not so large in size. The care put into the design of each floor, however, was what I believed would truly catch the hearts of all who visit. This, in turn, would be the greatest force forming the people's sense of connection to the space in the future.

A sound, healthy commercial facility should be one with a sense of intimacy and love felt by the customers who visit, its staff, the local people and all others. It may be likened to a tree with roots that gradually extend down and take root in the soil. My hopes for this design were that the Marronnier Gate would also become an indispensable presence, sprinkling its charms throughout Ginza. ×

Where **Tokyo, Japan**
When **September 2007**
Project type **Commercial Facility**
Photographer **Nacasa & Partners**
Architect **Taisei Corporation**

MARRONNIER GATE

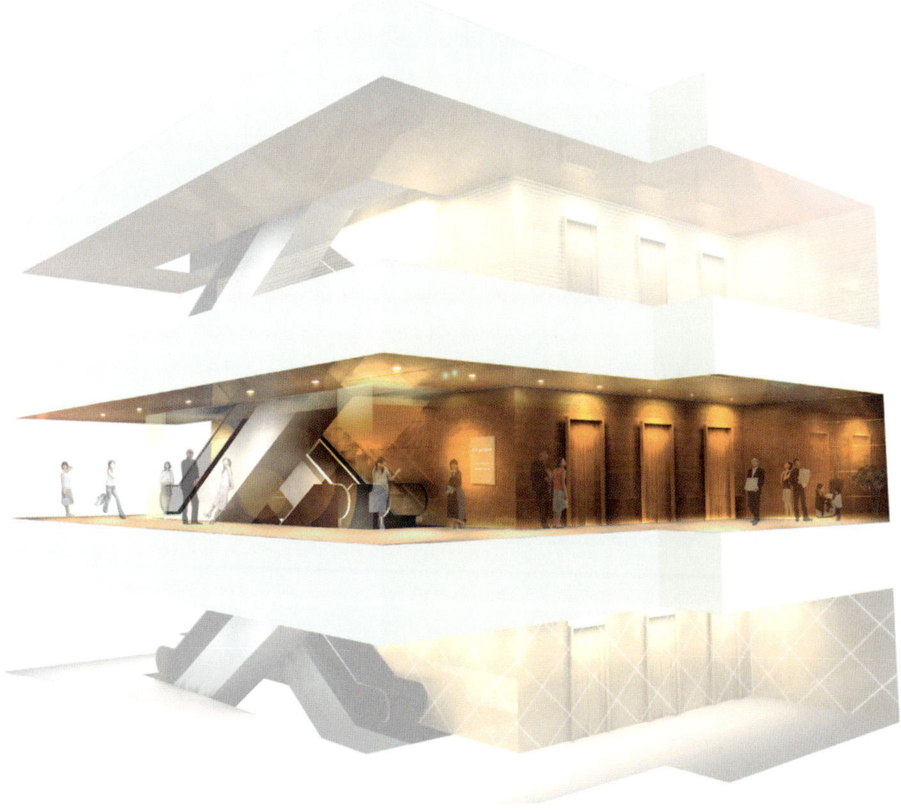

'The building is likened to a tree, taking root in the soil'

Toda Medical Healthcare Centre

The Toda Medical Healthcare Centre is a facility that provides precise and advanced medical examinations for its patients. My design here centred on the first floor entrance hall, the core of the facility, the fourth floor relaxation corner and the fifth floor chairman's room.

In the first floor entrance hall, a zone called the memorial corner joins the basic zones of the reception and waiting area. The memorial area contains an exhibition of founder Takatoshi Nakamura's achievements and social relationships. I selected three shades of wood for the three-zone space. A light-toned white ash was used in the waiting area, cherry was used for the front reception and walnut was used to produce a refined look in the memorial corner. In terms of form, lines and thin surfaces were adopted to create a light impression in the waiting room corner, while the memorial corner was designed for a sense of impressive weight.

The fourth floor relaxation area was a space for resting in between medical checkups. Sofas were specifically designed for this purpose, placed in an orderly alignment in the limited space. The seating here was designed to exist as spatial components, rather than big, heavy entities themselves.

The colours and fabric for the seating were chosen based on three types of materials and tones, extracted from the two kinds of flooring and fixtures. While each takes the same form, these three types of fabrics were scattered throughout to create a three-dimensional patchwork that melts into the space.

The fifth floor chairman's office is used not only as a workspace but also as a guest room. A display shelf was therefore installed upon the wall to provide rich colour and variation to the space. Adjacent to the office is a green roof, used also as a relaxation space that provides a sense of refreshment to those who visit and use the facility.

I have heard that since the opening of the centre, it has been frequented not only by locals but by those from a wider radius as well. People visit the facility not only for medical examinations, but to sit at the tables and enjoy pleasant conversation or to relax on a sofa lost in thought. In this way, a facility opened to the city exceeds its basic functions in an admirable way. ×

Where **Saitama, Japan**
When **February 2010**
Project type **Clinic**
Photographer **Satoshi Asakawa**

'My design created a three-dimensional patchwork that melted into the space'

Waiting area displayed art work.

The view of main entrance hall.

'In terms of form, lines and thin surfaces were adopted to create a light impression'

Memorial corner installed water sculpture beside window.

'I have heard that the centre exceeds its basic functions in an admirable way'

Chairman's office used as a guest room.

‘I selected three shades of wood for the three-zone space’

Relaxation area lined with patchworked sofas.

Chair for Toda Medical Healthcare Centre

This chair was designed for the Toda Medical Healthcare Centre, placed in a corner of the space lined with sofas. The sofas incorporated a three-dimensional patchwork, perhaps better expressed as a colour composition of fabrics. The chair introduced here was also designed along these lines.

The first thing I considered was how the chairs could exist in the space as spatial components. For this, I reinterpreted the two kinds of flooring as two kinds of colour and further translated this into fabric. The wood used for the sofa fixtures were also reinterpreted in the wood used for the chairs.

I did not try to make a relaxing space simply because of its relation to medicine, nor did I try to create a hotel lounge environment. Instead, I wanted my design to make the medical facility's environment as comfortable as possible. Above all, I strove to create a space that would be loved by its users for years to come. It would be my greatest joy as a designer to succeed in achieving a space that even slightly lightens the oppressive mood. ×

When **2010**
Project type **Seating**
Photographer **Satoshi Asakawa**

A Life

A strong awareness of the local area's unique qualities was what guided the interior design work for this project. Shops owned by an individual owner tend to reflect the tastes and ideals of that individual. However, in this space, I consciously adopted an approach of extracting the design by taking on an objective perspective, setting the theme as the lingering reverberations of the local area.

The overall composition of this space was separated into the styling, shampoo and backyard zones. While there were also bathroom, waiting room and reception spaces, this design progressed first from establishing the three main zones.

Individual seats with a heightened sense of privacy look onto a structural wall built-up to create volume as well as colourful elements, like the green on the ceiling, inspired by the colour of young leaves on a *sakura* (cherry blossom) tree. The shelf on the wall holds the mirrors and functions as a di play that brightens the space. The additional cherry pink colour helps to create the feel of a fleeting pastel world.

The countertop area in the styling zone also uses cherry pink in its most natural form. The ceiling is purposefully kept low to provide intonations in the space, so this gives the impression of higher ceiling heights in the other areas.

The ceiling in the shampoo area is designed on the image of *sakura* in full bloom, with the colour used to express both lightness and power and ribbed materials used to conjure the image of wind. The dyed cherry material of the furniture symbolises a tree trunk and the tiles covering a section of the wall represent the earth's energy.

The Japanese people's lifestyle was originally founded on an understanding of the local climate and a respect for it in their explorations of the best possible mode of living. The wooden frames of buildings, paper partitions, eaves with deep overhangs and the unique forms and materials of the roof are all indigenous designs perfected by each of the local regions.

In modern times, the abundance of equipment may render it unnecessary to create such traditional spaces. However, when we think about how mankind shall live hand-in-hand with the earth, we realise the need for an approach with a deeper connection to nature. ×

Where **Tokyo, Japan**
When **August 2009**
Project type **Salon**
Photographer **Satoshi Asakawa**

‘Colourful elements are inspired by the colour of young leaves on a cherry blossom tree’

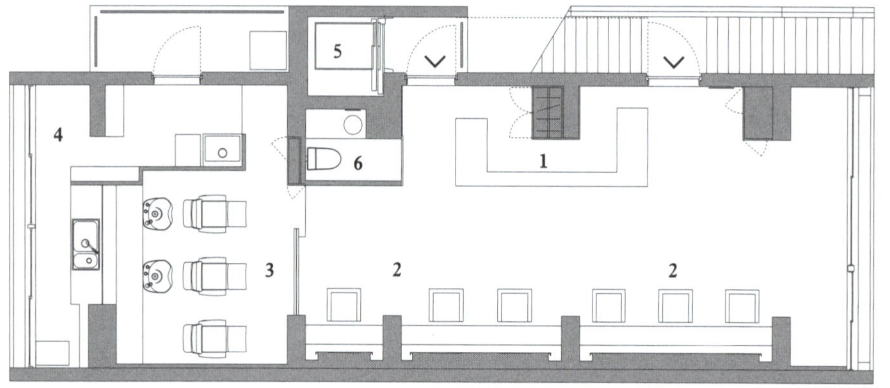

Floor Plan

1. Reception
2. Styling area
3. Shampoo area
4. Staff room
5. Elevator
6. Toilet

Minato Pharmacy Flagship Store

Minato Pharmacy is a dispensing pharmacy, where prescriptions are prepared and the necessary drugs are distributed to customers. Over-the-counter (OTC) medication is also sold here and, because it is a place frequented by a large group of people from the local community, it has both a commercial and a public character.

One of the distinct characteristics of a pharmacy is that it is a place to build trust amongst local people. Medicine helps bring people closer to a healthy state of equilibrium, and a pharmacy is a place for dispensing this.

Most people who visit pharmacies have health problems or are concerned about their health, so keeping visits short may be advisable, before exiting quickly for a breath of fresh air. In this way, a pharmacy differs from a typical commercial facility.

One final requirement of a pharmacy is the need for an open margin of space. As national policies may force the pharmacy to respond to reforms in its system or change its availability of OTC drugs, there is a possibility of future interventions in the physical 'hard' space of the pharmacy. I therefore considered it necessary for the space to respond flexibly to such conditions.

With these three main factors in mind, my interior design work progressed with considerations of some basic matters. Most pharmacies that take prescriptions typically have a dispensary located to the far end away from the entrance. However, in this design, I questioned whether this was truly the best answer from the standpoints of those who visit and locals who have yet to visit. One of my solutions was thus to locate the dispensary facing the street.

I also adopted two further concrete design methods. One was to communicate a memorable form to the city. Based on the image of an old, drawer-style medicinal cabinet, I designed a form reminiscent of drawers on the wall as a spatial icon.

The other method was the composition of colour placed at random across the floor. I used an inexpensive material here called vinyl composition tiles, but added the extra effort of cutting them from the manufacturer's predetermined sizes. This was an attempt to change the value of an inexpensive item through the power of design. This project was truly a piece of work made possible only through the cooperation of the craftsmen who worked tirelessly to complete the work. ×

Where **Tokyo, Japan**
When **April 2005**
Project type **Pharmacy**
Photographer **Satoshi Asakawa**

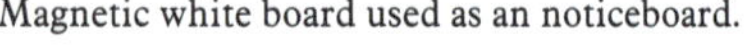

Magnetic white board used as an noticeboard.

Display shelf inspired from old drawer-style medicinal cabinet.

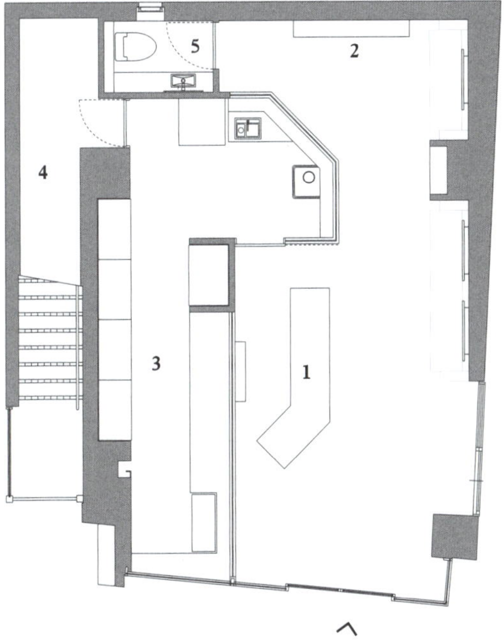

Floor Plan

1. Counter
2. Product display area
3. Dispensary
4. Stockroom
5. Toilet

'I designed a spatial icon reminiscent of an old, drawer-style medicinal cabinet'

Exhibition of New Textile Works by Kawashima Textile Manufacturers #2

In 2002, Kawashima Textile Manufacturers, one of the leading traditional textile manufacturers in Japan, held its first solo exhibition of new works under the theme of 'the potential of textiles for the future'. I came to be involved in the project as a spatial designer for the exhibition when consulted by a friend of mine, who was an in-house textile designer at the time.

The circular atrium stretching upward from the floor created a high-ceilinged space that was perfect for showing the dynamic strength of cloth. Here, I wanted to create a light and refreshing feel by selecting only the company's new white products and positioning them in a circle, nestled within the space. Being in a space enclosed by cloth enables us to feel not only the delicate and bodily tenderness of the material, but also an overwhelming power that is beyond our imagination.

In this project, I was able to unveil the hidden aspects of a company through spatial design. We must not forget that designing means fully understanding the hidden nature of the client and putting this into a visual form. This project helped us reaffirm that designing for a company involves looking back upon the company's history and creating a guide into its future. ×

Where **Tokyo, Japan**
When **December 2001**
Project type **Exhibition**
Photographer **Satoshi Asakawa**

Figure of a Woman

This chair, with a seat 240-mm wide, a depth of 270 mm and a height of 600 mm, was designed and created as an experiment to test the extent of change that people can endure in a chair's dimensions without experiencing discomfort.

There is an overabundance of information relating to chairs in the world today. Some sources recommend the sizes of chairs from an engineering perspective, some from an ergonomic angle. This chair was made as an antithesis to such current conditions. Although I have no statistical proof, it did not seem as though there were many negative opinions upon sitting in the seat. Rather, it seemed the one potential problem was that many wondered whether it was okay to sit in the chair, due to their first impressions of the design.

This chair, assembled mainly with transparent acrylic, is decorated with an abstract silk-screen print of a woman's silhouette. This design was inspired by the similarity I noticed between the chair seen from behind and the figure of a standing woman. The photo that was used was one that I found while skimming through a photography journal. When I contacted the publisher and communicated my intent, they willingly offered to cooperate, arriving at this design after overcoming various legal issues. ×

When **1999**
Project type **Seating**
Photographer **Satoshi Asakawa**

Yaeko Watanabe Exhibition

Traditional handicrafts passed down from the Edo period teaches us some important things that may have been forgotten in present-day society. What I mean by this is that the most important mindset in *monozukuri* (the art of making things) is to create things that are strong and durable, but our current lifestyles may have robbed us of our spirit of loving and caring for things. Thus, what is needed now may be the capability to learn from tradition and apply it to our own lifestyles in a manner suited to our times.

I visited the studio of Tsurezure many times in preparation for this exhibit. Countless pieces of handicraft examples could be found in rows and rows of tightly packed boxes. While our sensitivity to the seasons has become diluted in our present age, the spirit of *monozukuri* possesses high awareness of the seasons. As one of the few countries experiencing clearly delineated seasons of spring, summer, fall and winter, Japan has a truly valuable culture. Due to its beauty, nature has been worshipped as divine, giving rise to a culture in which the seasons are used in songs and haiku poetry. In this studio, I was able to glimpse this very basic *monozukuri* and was hit anew with the realisation that *monozukuri* with a love for nature and a sensibility to the seasons was not something the Japanese had treasured vehemently in their lifestyles, but was more an activity carried out naturally in daily life.

For the design of this exhibit, I attempted to carefully display the delicately constructed handicrafts one by one, imbued with the energy of a collective group. To this end, a stand was created at the centre of the space with folding white cubes. The height of these cubes increased towards the central point, enabling each piece to be viewed more easily. The varying heights of the stand each contained a separate view and a small universe of its own. The heights were designed so that viewers, from adults to children, could enjoy just the right amount of distance with the piece they were viewing.

Styrofoam was the material chosen for the stand. The choice of the material came from the fact that, this cool and manmade material seemed best suited for vividly displaying the pieces that Watanabe-san had created with all her heart and soul. Another factor for this choice of material was also its recyclability. This was not due to strong ecological awareness but because, having examined Watanabe-san's *monozukuri* philosophy, I wanted the exhibit space to assume as much of this philosophy as possible. This project was thus one in which I took on the task of design with a modern material, taking care not to deviate from the spirit of *monozukuri*. ×

Where **Tokyo, Japan**
When **November 2009**
Project type **Exhibition**
Photographer **Satoshi Asakawa**

Stool for Pleats Please Issey Miyake

A space can change dramatically based on the seating aspects and how they are arranged inside. In my realised interiors for Pleats Please Issey Miyake, the designs of the hanger racks and fixtures change largely based on the shop's spatial design.

This stool, however, has remained unchanged. While some minor adjustments have been made, such as the material and colour suited to the environment, and the seat height adjusted to the country's specifications, no changes have been made to its fundamental form.

The frame was made from stainless steel pipes with a mirror finish to match the hanger rack. The structural pieces have a diameter of 12 mm and, in areas where the pipes connect, the connecting pipe has a slightly thinner diameter. This creates a beautiful finish for the pipe joints. Two diameters of pipe (9 and 6 mm) were employed in this part of the design.

The seat cover is made of a white, flat material. While easily-used materials – like vinyl, leather, etc. – were originally selected, durable materials took their place after considering the requirement for the chair to be able to remain in use for as long as possible.

I feel that the image of people sitting down on the stool and resting one foot on the footrest creates the best relationship for showing people and the chair in the most beautiful light. ×

When **2003**
Project type **Seating**
Photographer **Satoshi Asakawa**

Yoyogi-Uehara House

The building here is built on a very narrow plot of land 5-m wide, yet stretching to a depth of 13 m. The most distinguishing feature of this land is its neighbouring retaining wall. My idea was thus to develop a positive understanding of the retaining wall and to actively incorporate it as a design element in the space. By employing exposed concrete in many areas of both the building and the interior, the concept envisioned here was the retaining wall melting into the building.

The biggest feature of the interior space is the V-shaped staircase stretching in the long direction from the first floor basement to the second floor. This staircase produces movement in the limited space. All rooms are connected to this staircase, optimising the flow of movement. The second floor is used as a living/dining space. A low window 10-m wide forms the aperture in the space. Light entering from the window reflects from the retaining wall and transforms into soft light. There are two rooms for kids located on the first floor, with large windows facing out onto the retaining wall. The first floor basement contains the main bedroom. The storage functions for all floors are collected in a core created at the centre of the space instead of by the exposed concrete walls, due to the possibility of condensation.

This was a truly meaningful project that questioned how to transform a 'negative' element for the better. ×

Where **Tokyo, Japan**
When **December 2005**
Project type **House**
Photographer **Masao Nishikawa**
Architect **Niizeki Studio**

'The concept envisioned the retaining wall melting into the building'

Borderless

This is a two-person bench. Made of a steel pipe frame, it has a slightly elevated seat and is equipped with a footrest. A lenticular seat is provided, with words appearing alternately in English and Arabic saying, 'Please sit down' and 'Take your time'.

There is no end to sorrow in this world. The hate displayed amongst fellow human beings and further acts of hatred strengthen this chain of evil. There are also a whole range of differing views the world over, for instance views on religion, on life and on the economy. People should intrinsically have the power to accept those with views different from their own. Unfortunately, the negative forces of the world work deep down and easily drown out the power of acceptance.

I do not often incorporate a political message in my designs. However, following the events of 11 September 2001, I decided to design with a social message on the current state of uncertainty towards the future. In the design of this bench, many people have responded and identified with the work's message, and the project became one in which I felt new possibilities of expanding my field of design in ways I had never imagined before. ×

When **2002**
Project type **Seating**
Photographer **Satoshi Asakawa**

TAKE YOUR TIME

Living involves sadness as well as joy. While there may be happy occasions, there may also be times when we cannot contain our anger. The word *ki-do-ai-raku* expresses the human emotions of joy, anger, pathos and humour in Japanese, but these emotions are by no means as easily reconcilable as the words suggest.

We enjoy a large collection of moments, from calm and soothing moments spent with family, special moments of quiet spent alone, to lively moments spent with friends. The spaces that human beings live in are always accompanied by a constantly flowing river of time. And because the world is always changing and vanishing, there is no such thing as permanency. This is truly a transitory world that we live in.

It may be strange but, because of this, I have always been conscious of creating *ba* (places) in my design that quietly envelop each moment of a person's life and respect that person's actions. Like the words *ba-sho* (space, as in location) and *gen-ba* (site), the word *ba* denotes a space where something exists or takes place. On the other hand, as seen in the words *ba-men* (scene) and *ba-ai* (a moment), it could also denote the situation, state or circumstances in which things are held. *Ba* does not simply apply to a particular space, but encompasses the flow of time and inner emotions of people. Perhaps thinking this through is what will bring us a step closer to the true nature of interior design.

It is the responsibility of those in the design field to think about what is or is not necessary, to determine what to continue or discontinue and to act upon these decisions. Reviving overlooked or forgotten values is another important role that design plays. Design is by no means solely about creating new things. ×

Chapter 3 × The Shape of Change

Pleats Please Issey Miyake

Bangkok Siam Discovery

This shop was the first branch of Pleats Please Issey Miyake in Thailand. Whenever I design spaces for brands where their products are sold, there are three directionalities that my thoughts can take. The first is for a design in which the space itself is assertive and memorable; the second is a design that expresses the brand's image through the use of the products' characteristics, employed as symbols throughout the space; and the third is a design devoted to becoming the products' backdrop, refraining from self-assertion and erasing its sense of presence. The developed markets of Pleats Please Issey Miyake in Japan, as well as Taiwan and Korea, are all based on this third directionality.

In the spatial design for this project, however, my design was based on the second category of expressing the brand image in the space, visualising the products' character in a spatial form. What I had in mind for this project was to understand the space itself as an important tool for communication and to communicate the product in an easily understandable way through the space. The products' outstanding characteristics, as can be seen in the brand's name, are their ridges made from pleating. Other qualities also include lightness, fast drying and wrinkle resistance.

Transparent glass delineates the shop from the corridor and a white entrance gate is formed from slicing into this line. The first things you see when you enter the space are the circular displays with their connections to the symbolic pillars. These displays come in three different sizes and heights, some with rotating capacities. The central space is gently partitioned by pipe hangers integrated into the vaulted roof, which is connected to the wall and further to the displays, forming an iconic interior element in the space. These loosely partitioned tube-like spaces create three different spheres.

Spatial designs for a globally-expanding national brand must answer to the demands of various countries and regions. In my designs, I have attempted to express the brand's qualities in relation to the particular country or region. I believe that it is the role of interior design to symbolically express a brand's products in spatial design and communicate its philosophy from various perspectives. ×

Where **Bangkok, Thailand**
When **July 2008**
Project type **Boutique**
Photographer **Satoshi Asakawa**

PLEATS
PLEASE

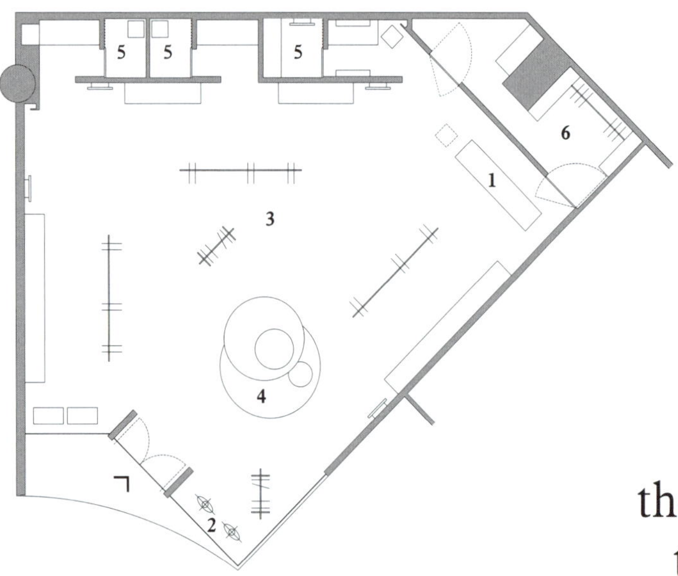

Floor Plan

1. Counter
2. Window display
3. Product display area
4. Display table
5. Changing room
6. Stockroom

'When designing a space, there are three directionalities that my thoughts can take'

'Pipe hangers integrated into the vaulted roof formed an iconic interior element'

Pleats Please Issey Miyake

Tainan Mitsukoshi

This shop is located in the basement floor of a department store. Usually in Japan, Pleats Please Issey Miyake stores are almost always located on the upper floors of the women's section of such commercial facilities, in relation to the brand's merchandising strategy.

In all of my spatial designs for Pleats Please Issey Miyake, I have always been conscious of creating a comfortable sense of tension, somewhat like the image of a perpetual flow of quiet time. When products are displayed based on the season's designs and composition, a quiet change arises within the shop. This can produce a gently flowing sense of time in one instance and a delightful impression in the next.

My thoughts when I visited the site before beginning the design were to fashion a space that, while tranquil, would also encompass a strength and dynamism rooted into the earth. Perhaps these ideas were derived from the humid climate of the region, the lack of natural light reaching the underground space, the spatial composition of narrow passages on the floor, and the configuration of nearby shops.

For the overall composition of the space, my image was of multiple cubes in varying volumes scattered randomly throughout the space, as if the cubes were drifting through space, frozen in time. We must not forget, however, that as a shop, it is also a place of business. The sizes and heights of these cubes were therefore decided one by one for their materiality and function. A number of cubes were positioned along the wall in order to sustain the image of being released from gravity. These cubes were thus arranged to provide a fluid balance of sizes and heights suited to the functions of the cubes.

Designing requires finding a solution to what is being designed. What is important here is the constructive repetition of *shikou* (thinking) and *shikou* (testing). Design requires the visualisation of carefully deliberated ideas from the world of imagination into the world of physical objects. It must not be kept within oneself but shared with many people, making it also important for people to identify with it. I believe that it is only when people have identified with the design that it begins to have a life of its own.

Spatial designs for the continually evolving Pleats Please Issey Miyake must be able to withstand long years of use without losing their luster. It is therefore important to apply layer upon layer of *shikou* (thinking) and *shikou* (testing). In this design, I made a conscious attempt to stray away from the direction of uniform results and unconsciously repetitive designs. ×

Where **Tainan, Taiwan**
When **May 2008**
Project type **Boutique**
Photographer **Chien Jung-Tsung**

PLEATS
PLEASE
ISSEY MIYAKE

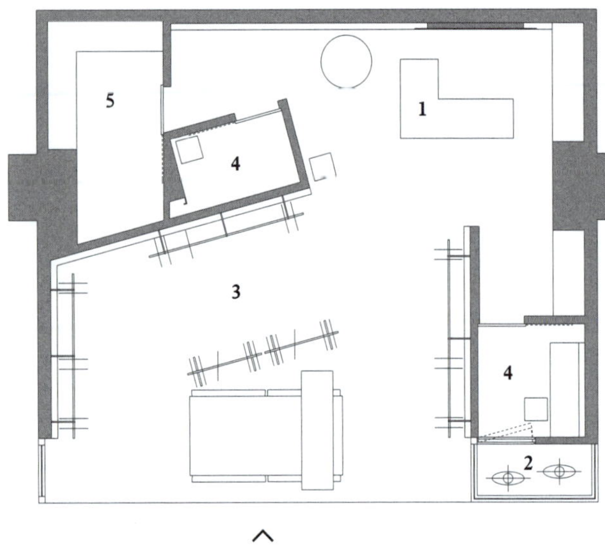

Floor Plan

1. Counter
2. Window display
3. Product display area
4. Changing room
5. Stockroom

'The cubes were drifting through space, frozen in time'

PLEATS PLEASE

Weather Forecast

The glass used in this chair is optical glass – a homogenous glass made from agitating melted materials and maintaining them in a pure state during production. It is a material used to transmit images through the reflection and refraction of light, and is now found in a variety of applications, such as cameras, telescopes and microscopes. In the production stage of optical glass, however, air bubbles may form or a phenomenon called 'striae' can occur, when a refractive index differs from its surroundings. When such events happen, the glass is disposed of as a defective product. The beauty of the material, however, remains intact. I felt that simply discarding this beauty would be too much of a waste. The design of this chair was thus born, not for any reasons of ecological awareness nor with any purpose to reuse a defective material, but simply because I wanted to give form to something I felt was beautiful.

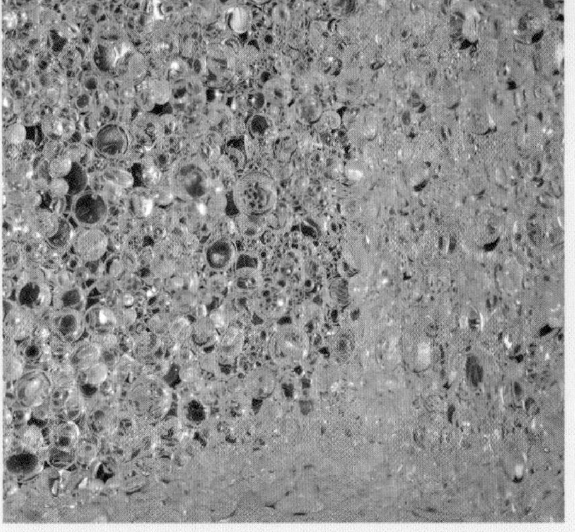

Leading on from my hunch that something could be done, adhesive techniques were investigated. Experimentation focused upon what would happen when it was bonded to a polished mirror surface or an acrylic board. This progressed, until I decided to take on the challenge of making a chair with the policy of limiting the material to glass whenever possible, and creating a piece in which the material's beauty could be felt at full force.

As the product required sufficient strength to hold different weights of people, this could not be secured by solely bonding glass to glass. Thus, transparent acrylic boards were combined to provide the necessary structure. The backrest, side plates on either side and the seat were formed from four sheets of 10-mm-thick acrylic boards, assuring the minimal function of sitting.

Once this chair had been created, I decided to reorganise and develop four kinds of chairs imagined from this glass. The keywords connecting these four chairs were weather states – 'sunny, cloudy, rainy and snowy'. By setting these keywords, the directionality to adopt for the design of the other three chairs became exceedingly clear. Other advantages for using these keywords were that they would help fashion the formal characteristics of the chair and that they would be easy design words for many people to identify with.

Realising a design in a prototype requires constantly overcoming various obstacles, not least securing the production fees. Only one prototype – cloudy – for this series has been realised thus far, and I am hoping for the day that I can complete the entire series. I do not know how long it will be, but I aim to continue designing with high hopes of revealing this series someday for all to see. ×

When **2009**
Project type **Seating**
Photographer **Satoshi Asakawa**

The prototype for the 'cloudy' chair was realised in 2009.

Renderings of the other family members in the Weather Forecast series (from left to right): sunny, rainy and snowy.

'I took on the challenge to create a piece in which the material's beauty could be felt at full force'

The production process involved afixing optical glass beads onto the acrylic base.

Pleats Please Issey Miyake

Chiayi Nice Matsuya

An elevation with three different expressions was created for this 100-m^2 space. The first was a show window facing out to people walking along the street. This space, closed in by glass, displays the brand's look for the season. The second was the open facade with the view of the entire shop, which can be seen from the main entrance of the department store. The third was the narrow, closed facade, with a closed entrance reminiscent of a *nijiriguchi* (the small entrance to a tea ceremony room). This facade was designed to line up with those of the other shops on the same floor. The glimpses of different scenes from the small entrance arouse curiosity. From the inside of the department store, the shop opens on two sides facing the shared hallway; the entrance and these two facades of different character were created for shaping the spatial characteristics of the shop.

As an interior design for a Pleats Please Issey Miyake shop, this space also focuses on the creation of a 'white backdrop'. White is a quiet colour that makes no strong assertions. Here, polarised paint for creating beautiful colour shifts was applied to the space as an attempt to create a new 'white'. While it may appear white at first glance, faint pinks and greens appear in the space depending on the perceived angle, producing a fleeting sense of colour.

Display shelves were located in the centre of the space. These scattered cubes fit together like pieces of a puzzle and exist in the space as symbolic interior elements.

The colours of the walls enveloping the space and the moveable fixtures have a relationship close to the complementary colours of soft pink and green. The finished space, may not provide a dynamic change in colour, but the quiet shift of colours will envelop your body and bestow upon you a sense of 'quiet beauty'.

The interior design here was an attempt at creating *ba* (place) through the harmonious presence of two opposing elements. Such presence of things and their consequential perceptions are largely based on their spatial relationship. This project was one that evolved from my idea that the presence of interior elements can complement one another to maintain a comfortable balance for people. ×

Where **Chiayi, Taiwan**
When **May 2006**
Project type **Boutique**
Photographer **Satoshi Asakawa**

PLEATS
PLEASE
ISSEY MIYAKE

‘I decided the shelves would exist in the space as symbolic interior elements’

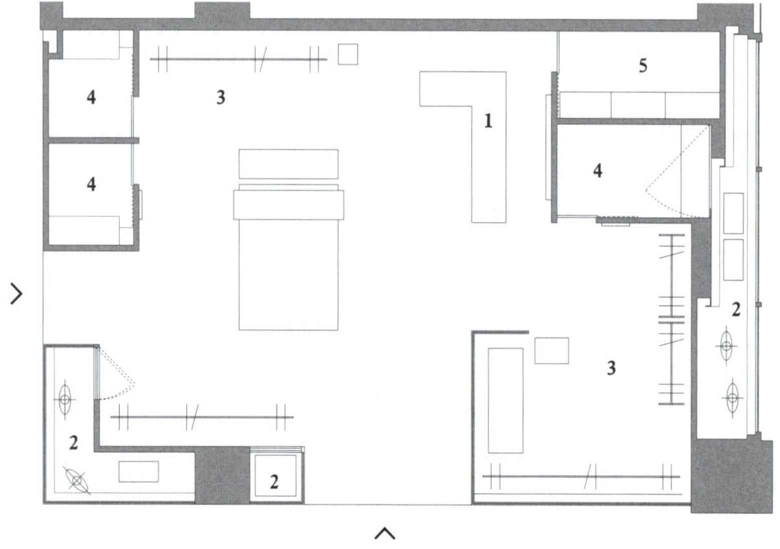

Floor Plan

1. Counter
2. Window display
3. Product display area
4. Changing room
5. Stockroom

Nobuko Nishida

The distinctive feature of this accessories shop was that, despite its small 20-m^2 size, it had two entrances. The alley behind the building was fully visible from the busy street in front. A counter for assisting customers and displaying products, plus a fitting room and toilet were all required in the space, and I could tell from an early stage that I would be encountering some problems in order to meet the brief. As I struggled to find solutions to these hurdles, there were three important considerations I made in developing my interior design.

The first was 'the look of a shop with two expressions'. I contemplated what kind of design solution would be necessary to make use of the characteristic double entrance in the space. So, I planned the entrance facing the alley in a more open character, with an unbroken view of the products to communicate the ambience in a direct way. In contrast, I created a very closed environment on the side facing the larger street, which was bustling with noise and laden with traffic. The aim here was to spark imagination in passers-by.

The second consideration was the 'creation of space with a height difference'. Cubes of varying scale overlapped one another through the space so that a change could be felt in the distance between the people and the products. I tried to create richer spaces by consciously creating changes in the vertical direction.

The third consideration was 'seven whites'. The basic tone of the space was white, composed of seven kinds of white materials. Imagining the sight of products placed in the space, I combined lustrous white with a contrasting matte white. In terms of texture, I chose a rough finish for colours with a lustrous shine. The shades were chosen based on the combination's balance in hue and brightness, like warm whites in contrast to cool whites in order to showcase the products. On the other hand, I consciously employed colour in the interiors of the drawers and storage, to create a mechanism in which colour appears in the space accompanying people's actions. Organisation is important in stocking products, thus, colour was used as a memory-evoking tool for increasing the ease of organisation within the shop.

The bags, made with reverence for the materials used and infused with new life through the hands of the artists, exude a modest but powerful expression out to the city. In my eyes, these bags appear as if they are waiting in the shop for the day they leave their nest. Realising a project, regardless of the difference in budget, time or scale, is an amazing task filled with a sense of joy. ×

Where **Tokyo, Japan**
When **April 2008**
Project type **Retail**
Photographer **Kanta Ushio**

Nobuko Nishida

‘I create richer spaces by consciously creating changes in the vertical direction’

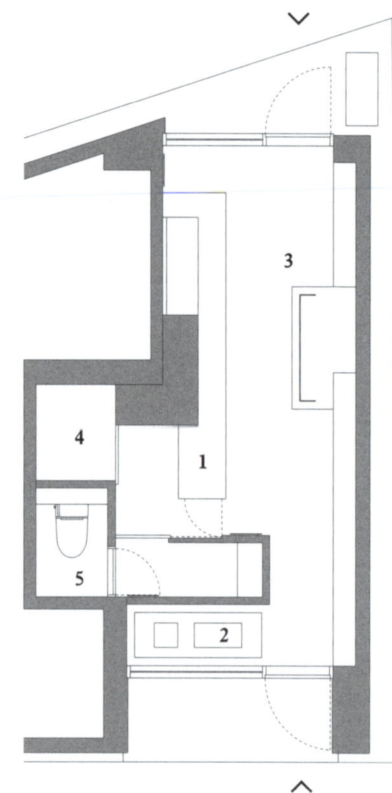

Floor Plan

1. Counter
2. Window display
3. Product display area
4. Stockroom
5. Toilet

Pleats Please Issey Miyake + me Issey Miyake

Seoul Hyundai Coex

Despite its limited area, this shop houses two brands in the same space – both Issey Miyake's latest Pleats Please collection and the 'me' brand. Due to these two different styles, requiring a space with different expressions, I was very conscious of creating an opposition that would bring out the individualities of both brands while maintaining a balance of their distinct personalities.

First, for a formal opposition, I differentiated the space through the use of lines and curves. For the Pleats Please side, I used lines to compose a sharp and sophisticated style; at the same time, for the 'me' side, I used curves for a lively, pop feel. Secondly, for the colour palette I focused on the opposites of 'calm versus activity'. On the Pleats Please side, I used indefinably ambiguous shades of white, blue and purple. On the 'me' side, I used a dynamic contrast of solid white and vibrant blue stripes.

Lastly, I considered the relationship between new and old materials, as a means of expressing opposing times and delineating the boundary between the interior, store space and the outside corridor. I used modern materials inside the shop but consciously retained stone materials embedded with the department store's history.

This was a project based on the idea that when 'opposing' things are made to 'coexist' giving rise to greater power. ×

Where **Seoul, Korea**
When **March 2008**
Project type **Boutique**
Photographer **Kim Kwang Ook**

PLEATS
PLEASE

PLEATS
PLEASE

ISSEY MIYAKE
me

Modigliani Nuca

There used to be a pottery shop called Tsuchi No Hana, located along a narrow street running parallel to Aoyma's Kotto-dori (Antiques Avenue). The interior elements of the space included the symbolic display in the centre, low walls and shelves encircling the space, and partitions for dividing the space. Further, the balance between these elements composed the space. The shop, subtly drawing out the charms of select works by exceptional artists, was memorable to passers-by and was firmly rooted in the local area. Opened in 1994, the shop regrettably closed its doors in 2007, after 13 years in business. However, Tsuchi No Hana then changed its line of business and reopened in October of the same year as a textile accessories shop called Modigliani Nuca.

With the change in line of products came a reconfiguration of space. A great deal of effort was exerted in renovating the spatial image by dramatically changing the materials, colours and details of the existing shop based on the goals of the space in terms of transparency, colour and lightness.

What was most important for me here, was to uphold the exemplary spatial design of Tsuchi No Hana before its renovation, and sustain the memories of passers-by. Thus, the light green facade, like a freestanding piece of coloured paper, provides a fresh and dignified atmosphere to an unsympathetic city. The colour of the interior, resembling the Japanese skin tone, rekindles one's imagination to envision wearing the products. Glass was used in the display stand at the centre of the space so that the products are seen through glass. The surrounding low walls and shelves were painted such that they integrated into the space, and the partitioning walls were made in see-through textiles that gave a feel of lightness to the space, different from before.

Design exists in close proximity to the fields of industry and economy. However, it would be much too disappointing if it were used only as a tool for such ends. While it is an effective means of rousing the market economy, if design itself becomes a commodity to be selected, expelled and consumed, we would then be losing sight of the true meaning of design. The business world often considers interior design as temporary; however, there are times when it survives longer than human beings. Therefore, this became a project in which I paid homage to an exemplary design and felt the importance of keeping it alive. This is something I would like to constantly be aware of when designing in the future as well. ×

Where **Tokyo, Japan**
When **October 2007**
Project type **Retail**
Photographer **Nacasa & Partners**

'What was most important for me was to sustain the memories of passers-by'

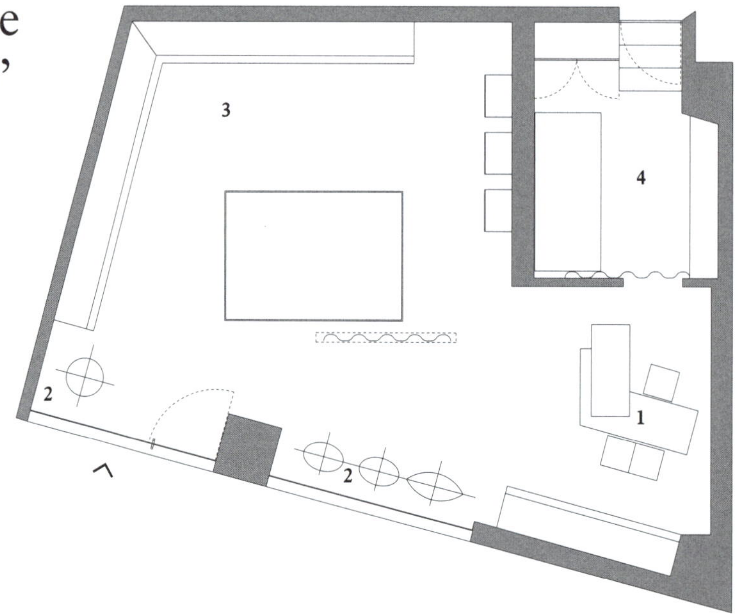

Floor Plan

1. Counter
2. Window display
3. Product display area
4. Stockroom

Minato Pharmacy

Higashi Kitazawa

Minato Pharmacy has a few branches in Tokyo. A new branch opened in Higashi Kitazawa in the Setagaya ward, following the renewal of the flagship store in Wakabayashi. Design manuals are typically created for the spatial design of brands with multiple branches, thereby unifying the colour, material, form and function of the different branches and working to assert the brand's image.

The Minato Pharmacy's branding through design, however, does not depend on a design manual. The company adopts a spatial brand design that does not overly rely on colour, material, form or function. Instead of layering upon its brand image, the design consists of linking like in a *renga* (poetic dialogue of linked verses). This is because the Minato team believes it is necessary to design each branch through the questioning of why it has to be a certain way.

In this spatial design, I adopted the use of four shades of warm colours seen in my earlier work. At the time of these prior works, I had cut up homogeneous tiles and laid them on the floor; this time, I randomly arranged porcelain tiles treated with four kinds of glaze on the full surface of the wall. My idea was that adapting the colours into a different element and reflecting this in the spatial design would connect the brand's image.

The various sizes of shelves placed on the wall, while seemingly random at first glance, were designed in height and depth based on the display and ease of picking up the products. At the same time, I also considered functionality, like chamfering corners for safety purposes. The ceiling was fully covered in wood film, leaving only a single area cut out in white for indirect lighting. Due to the lack of high ceiling space, I also considered the layout of typically hidden areas like air-conditioning equipment and ducts.

I secured space for an almost overly large counter set in the middle of the space. This was because, even with such a limited amount of space, I wanted to create time for unrushed dialogue with customers.

I believe that the interior design of Minato Pharmacy will gradually begin to unveil its framework as more and more branches are built. This may be considered something like a gentle procession of design. What design elements to link together and what concepts to carry on to the future – these are issues that I shall continue to speculate. ×

Where **Tokyo, Japan**
When **September 2010**
Project type **Pharmacy**
Photographer **Satoshi Asakawa**

'The design consists of a poetic dialogue of linked verses'

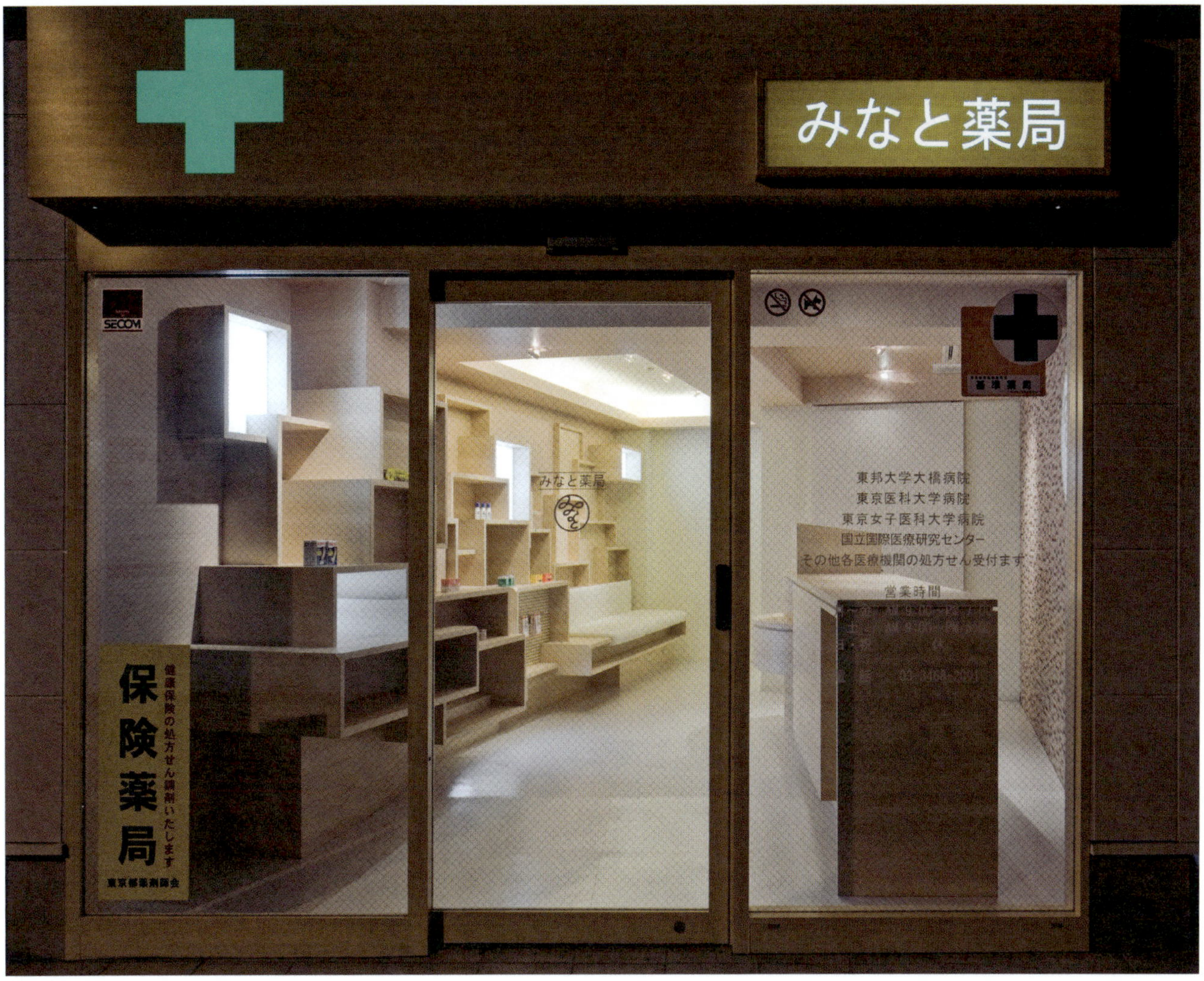

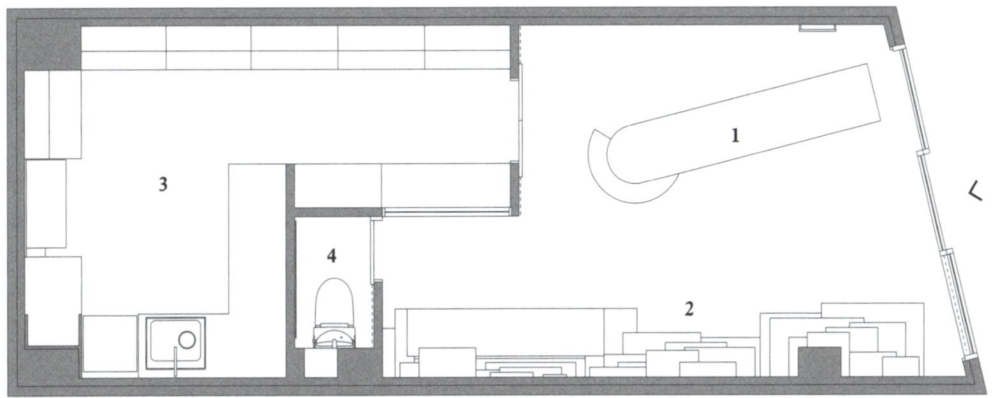

Floor Plan

1. Counter
2. Product display area
3. Dispensary
4. Toilet

コーラック

Beveled Edge

Removing the sharp edges of a product by chamfering them can help improve safety, and it also results in a 'softer' image, realising a beautiful object. Although it may be a trifling detail, it has the power to greatly change the entire presence of the object.

The chair and side table introduced here were based on the idea of showing the act and process of chamfering as a design element. The composition used 25 x 25 mm square pieces in differing lengths. Although cubes and other rectangular volumes come in all different sizes, they each always have 12 edges. These edges were cut at 45-degree angles to create an approximately 4-mm surface.

The square bars were first painted red and then chamfered so that when a surface is cut diagonally, the natural wood material is visible. A dowel was then used to glue and solidify the form. The side table next to the chair was matched to the height of the chair's arm. The second rack was also set to the height of the chair seat. In this way, the chair and side table were not created individually – rather, the project's focus was on the creation of a comfortable balance between the two. ×

When **2013**
Project type **Seating**
Photographer **Satoshi Asakawa**

2 pm in the Autumn

Have you ever noticed how frequently you see chairs from behind in your everyday life? Chairs are seen at the dining table at home, in the conference room at work and, for students, in classrooms and libraries. It is actually no exaggeration to say that the back of a chair determines its impression. As a result of this, I often design chairs thinking about how to show its figure from behind.

The chair introduced here was originally a dining chair designed for a close friend of mine since high school. The family needed a dining set when they bought their new home and so I designed a dining table and chairs to go with it. The materials I used included soft-grained maple and durable amber-coloured vinyl leather. I often try to pursue experimental designs but in this home, my focus was for the furniture to naturally meld into the home.

As for the chair's form, the seat was fashioned in a trapezoidal shape with the legs closer together in the back than in the front. I further considered how to hide the connecting ties between the back legs when seen from behind, as this would help the seat feel higher. The thinner frame and high positioned seat was designed to provide a gentler touch. ×

When **2001**
Project type **Seating**
Photographer **Satoshi Asakawa**

Throughout my career, I have never really put complicated thought into design. In my interior design work, I have always been conscious of supporting people's livelihoods. This includes the *ba* (places) of daily life like the home, or the slightly showy *ba* for selling products. The chairs, tables and lighting fixtures used therein are also pertinent in the creation of *ba*. While the designed space, line of business or product may differ, I believe that there is no difference or disconnect in my attitude toward design. This is because the concept of making *ba* (places) for people's activities lies deep within my soul.

However, when working in the field of interior design, I have come to the realisation that some things just cannot be glossed over – for instance, the creation of social foundations that support an energy-saving lifestyle, considerations of the environment including the effective use of materials and the problem of processing scraps. Although the purpose of design lies not just in providing answers to society, there are many issues that I cannot ignore as an active designer in our world today.

In society, interior design for commercial spaces – which lies in close proximity to the industrial world – can be mercilessly buried into the mechanisms of the economy. Even if the space is durable, evaluated highly for its design quality, recognised as a *ba* (place) that is greatly loved by its users, the cold, harsh truth is as follows: if it does not contribute to economic activities, it cannot be accepted. This is why I undertake experimental projects and engage in design with a desire to leave a small foundation for the future. ×

Chapter 4 × The Persuit of Possibilities

999+1

Not a day goes by in our everyday lives where we do not interact with 'numbers'. The first thing we do when we wake up in the morning is to look at the clock. When waiting at the bus stop, we look for our usual bus marked with the usual number. In the car, we glance at the radio tuner to find our favourite station's frequency. Without even realising it, we are constantly in tune with numbers, day in and day out.

I was always attracted to this numerical world, ever since I was a young boy. Taking on seemingly impregnable problems not only challenged my mind but also uplifted my emotions. The unravelling of the grand scheme of things through the process of problem-solving and the unyielding sense of exhilaration when reaching the solution, gave me an incredibly rewarding feeling.

The title of this work, '999+1', comes from its form made using 999 spheres. Spheres were the only shape I used in the formation of the piece. In other words, the piece is made from 999 spheres joined together. The '+1' here refers to the one light source that is added to this. The spheres are stacked together to create a silhouette of the lampshade and its base, and the design process began with deciding on the outline of the final product. The lampshade has a diameter of 20 cm and height of 40 cm. The base supporting the lampshade is in a disk shape with an approximately 15-cm diameter, and the post is a cylinder 5 cm in diameter. This outline was determined by adjusting the volume of the form; the form, in turn, was created using a 3D printer.

Engaging in design also means constantly confronting the various problems that appear before us. I have attempted to design each time with a desire to exact a clear solution, just as if I were finding the solution to a mathematical problem. Like clearing away the fog, I have strived towards a definitive answer, and I believe that I have successfully arrived at these solutions.

However, as the days pass, I sometimes find myself lost in the quandary of design, questioning my other self on my design work and whether or not the answer I had sought so striven to find was truly the right one. This may be what it means to design. I know that I will find the difficulty and profundity of design constantly within myself now and in the future. ×

When **2007**
Project type **Light**
Photographer **Satoshi Asakawa / Nacasa & Partners**

'I stacked 999 spheres to look like a lamp, with the addition of +1 bulb'

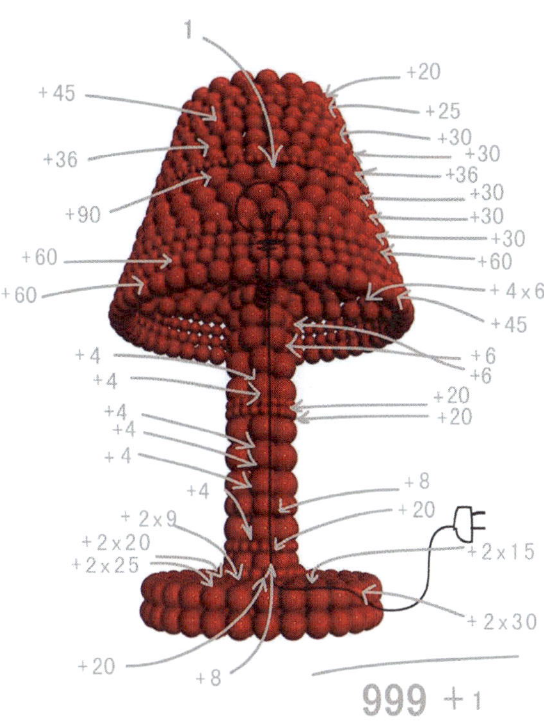

Moon River

This product design series was created through 'rapid prototyping'. A number of 3D printing centres are now found in the city, with easily accessible 3D printers. If this could increase the strength and variety of materials with which we engage in creative activity or expand the size of our creations, it will become an indispensable item to our lives and may even come to shoulder the development of a new lifestyle.

Although technical talk has taken precedent so far, what I wanted to create with this light fixture was an ethereal light, like 'moonlight' seeping into daily life. The aim of this design was to recreate moonlight, which has enraptured the hearts of many since olden times, using modern-day technology. The keyword 'moonlight' led to a spherical design reminiscent of a full moon, with slits cut into this round moon-like shape to create shadows. This was a form derived from the image of craters. While it may be difficult to decipher without an explanation, these slits are words that have been stretched horizontally. Shifting your eyes to the top portion will enable you to read the words. If you look inside these slits, you will see a cylindrical post with a mirror finish standing in the centre of the sphere. The slits outside reflect onto this post, and the words to the famous song, Moon River, appear here.

While it is a simple spherical shape at first glance, the design of this light fixture was experimental in terms of its process of formation and painting. Polarised paint, for reflecting and refracting colours based on viewing and lighting angle, has been applied on the surface. With differing angles of incidence, the ensuing wavelengths change to create varying colours.

With the advent of countless designs and formal expressions made using digital tools, we inevitably encounter talk of the appeal of natural materials or the marvels of handmade objects. It is not which is superior to the other that we should be debating here.

There are some designs that cannot be derived without the use of digital tools, while some are made possible only through the memory ingrained in human hands. Both are highly captivating and both can be said to contain some shortcomings. I believe that developing a deeper understanding of these will expand the world of design dramatically. This project was one in which I attempted a design that could not have been arrived at without the use of digital tools. ×

When **2007**
Project type **Light**
Photographer **Nacasa & Partner**

'The words to the song, Moon River, appear inside the light'

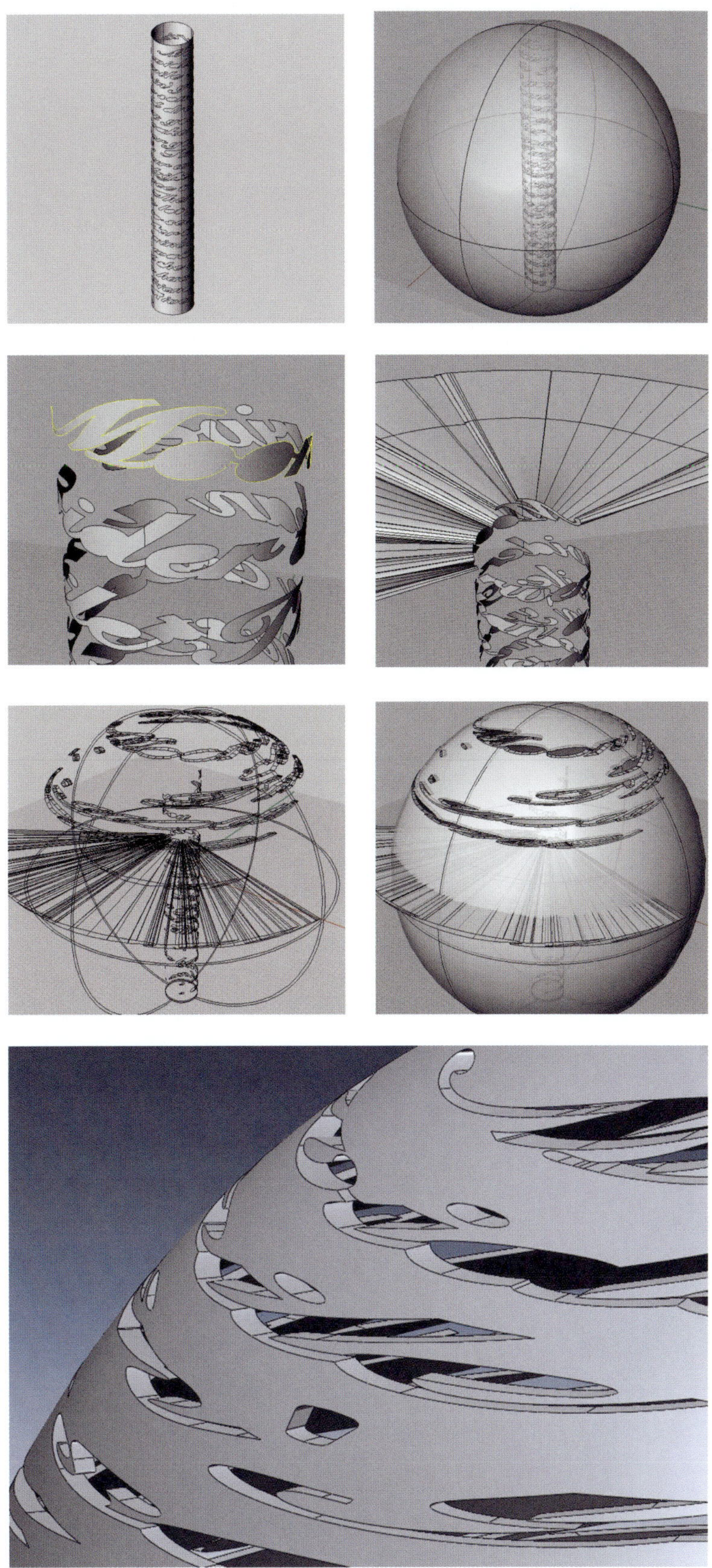

In order to show the words of the song,
the surface slits were designed using 3D data.

Wrapping Chair

In Japan, you often see pears, peaches, apples and other fruits wrapped carefully in a styrofoam mesh material at markets. As it can also function as a cushioning material, styrofoam has been used for a number of delicate materials in recent times. I felt a new possibility of form in this simple structure with its material flexibility and ability to mould itself into any shape. I thus developed my design with this material in mind, striving for a form that could be used for a person to comfortably sit in.

There are two variations to this product: one with an opening stretching through the foot of the chair to the back, and the other from the seat to the floor. This was my first attempt at creating an object for sitting where I used a 3D printer. There was a limit to the maximum size that could be printed at the time, so it was impossible to print the form in a single mould in Japan. I thus conducted research thinking of divisible proposals. In the end, I altered the scale and realised these proposals as studies of form.

Through structural calculations of pipe diameter, pitch and materials, I found solutions to provide the minimum requirements for strength and function, enabling people to sit on the chairs comfortably. ×

When **2007**
Project type **Seating**
Photographer **Satoshi Asakawa**

First prototypes produced by 3D printer.

'I felt a new possibility of form in this simple structure'

Visuals to illustrate the inspiration for this chair concept.

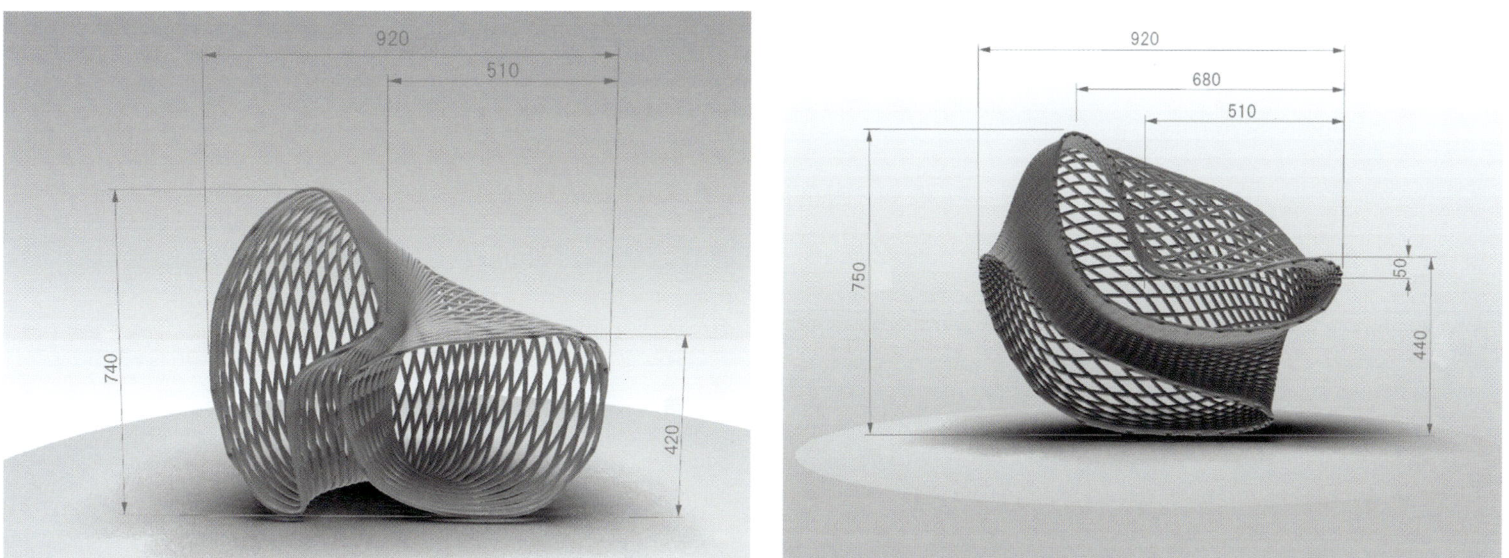

Study renderings investigating the possible dimensions for the chair.

Endless

Here I made a light fixture by giving form to a stream of words, written in English. The words for all of the months of the year, from January to December, are repeated from the top of the form, spiralling down around its outer periphery. When the words reach the bottom, they begin to cover the underside of the lamp, and then, wrapping around the centre post, they start to move upward in the same spiral format.

The overall silhouette was formed based on the image of a table lamp familiar to most people. The form itself has no strong message, and the process is one that is used to express the design concept in a clear manner.

This was my first design based on the use of a 3D printer. When I first created this, my idea was to use a light bulb as the light source; however, times have changed, and the use of LED lights as a light source has become much more familiar to us today.

If I were to reconsider the design now, the dimensions of the light source may be subject to change. Therefore, this design work shall continue to change in form, responding to changes in our light sources. ×

When **2002**
Project type **Light**
Photographer **Satoshi Asakawa**

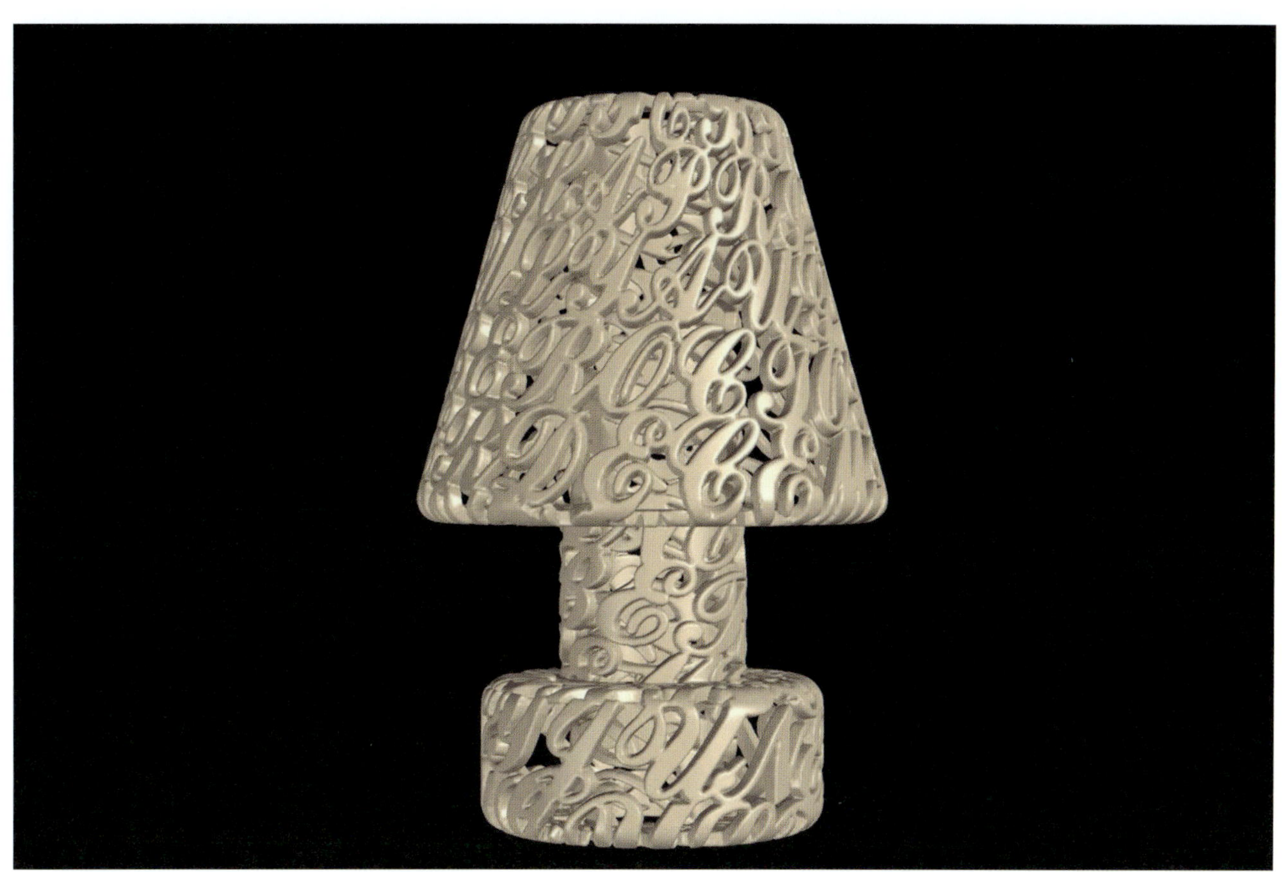

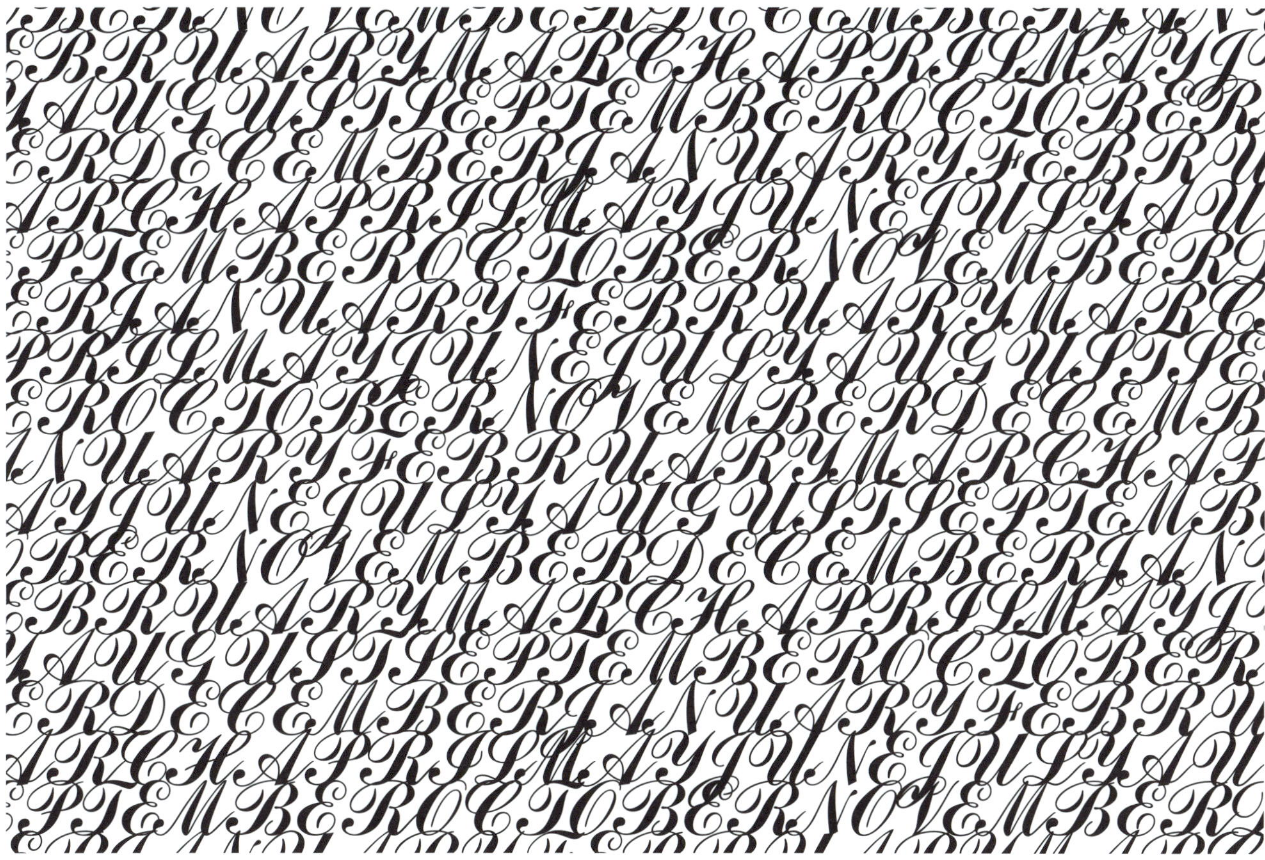

Kariya Highway Oasis

I became involved in this project as an interior designer because of a request from an architect friend from my school days. I was responsible for the interior design for a shopping centre, located at the heart of the Kariya Highway Oasis – a commercial facility where motorists can take a rest from driving.

I decided to use the project's scale to its advantage to develop two different kinds of materials. In most cases, I usually choose materials straight out of manufacturer's catalogue when developing my spatial design. As this project covered a wide expanse of area, I was able to use semi-custom-ordered materials without burdening manufacturers on the issues of production process or cost.

One of these materials included flooring material made of vinyl composition tiles. I used nine different kinds of colour patterns imagined from the word 'oasis'. I tried various combinations, created samples and devised a presentation with these materials placed in a model. Furthermore, I visited a factory overseas for the production of materials, which were then realised after processes such as the final confirmation of colour matching. Difficulties in this design started at the formulation of the initial idea and later continued with the acceptance of the proposal: keeping it within the budget and ensuring that it met the deadline. Through my passionate efforts, I fortunately found many people who also expended their unsparing efforts in order to realise the creation of these materials.

Film sheets were used on the walls to aid circulation, made in a three-layer structure. One of these layers is a base colour for producing a texture close to that of natural wood. The second is a sheet for expressing the wood grain, and the last is a surface film for enhancing its sense of reality. These layers are coated one on top of the other and, while each of these simply appear to be a piece of sheet material, there is a quality that can only be found through their layering.

Here, I created a material that possessed a unique quality – as if the lustre of metal was fused with the natural materiality of wood. While both materials are familiar to us in our everyday lives, I thought that by combining the two, I would be able to transform it into an unfamiliar material. While the material may look like wood at first glance, as the morning or evening light infiltrates the room, a shine that does not exist in wood appears. This was an attempt not at pursuing the authenticity of wood or metal but at achieving a new expression possible only through a manmade material. ×

Where **Aichi, Japan**
When **December 2004**
Project type **Rest Area**
Photographer **Koji Horiuchi**
Architect **Tetsuya Ukai Architects**

本格派たこ焼き
KARIYA HIGHWAY OASIS
宝くじ
circle-k
ラーメン
横綱

'I created a unique material where lustre of metal was fused with the natural materiality of wood'

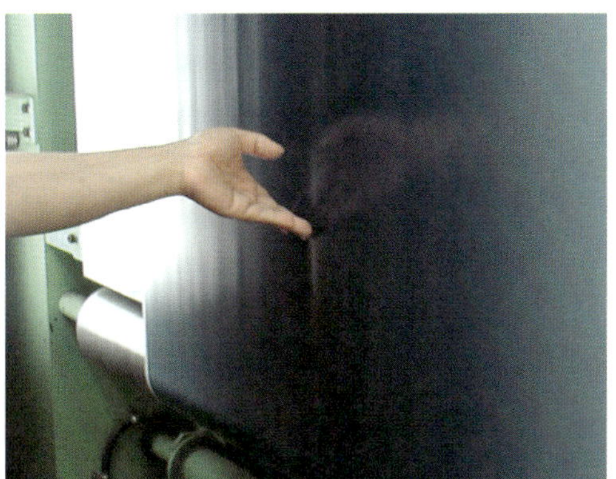

Sample of various combinations of colours and production of the film.

La Jeune

Belle Vie Akasaka

When the second La Jeune shop opened in Akasaka, what I attempted was a spatial design with a new expression, pursuing the concept of the 'presence of beauty' produced by the space itself.

In the original La Jeune shop that I designed the previous year, I experimented with covering the entire space in aluminum. At this second shop, I opted to use decorative melamine boards to cover the space. These boards are strong and highly resistant to heat, water, weather, wear and damage.

In this project, the brand's beautiful woman motif was used on the surface of these decorative boards. An important thing to note here is that the material was not made simply by sticking on printed sheets to the boards but by laminating the printouts onto the boards to fashion them into strong building materials. They are thus durable enough to be used on the countertops, and considering the cleaning and maintenance work necessary for continued use, they are clearly different in quality as compared to printed sheets.

This material was used on the walls, furniture and counters throughout the space as an interior element series. Here, instead of simply showing a visual image, I disassembled the visual reference and reassembled it to pursue the ideal of the 'presence of beauty'. I thus decided on an intermediary visual design somewhere between concrete and abstract, using a monotone world expressing only through dark and light tones of a single colour. I sometimes feel an unfathomable power in a monotone world that cannot be seen in works composed of many colours – perhaps this is because it demands the imagination of its viewers.

In the creative business, there will always be undesirable conditions like limitations and constraints as the project progresses. What is necessary to continue the act of creation under such conditions is a clear vision of what you yearn to accomplish.

In the world of spatial design, we can reveal hidden possibilities and attractive features in everyday objects simply by changing the way we view them. The means of exposing such hidden features involves clearly extracting the special factors and building upon them or, alternatively, minimising any or all of its negative aspects. Building material manufacturers also strongly agreed with the significance of such endeavours. Therefore, this became a project in which we attuned ourselves to the hidden possibilities around us and engaged in the potentials of the material. ×

Where **Tokyo, Japan**
When **November 2000**
Project type **Retail**
Photographer **Satoshi Asakawa**

La Jeune

La Jeune
La Jeune
La Jeune

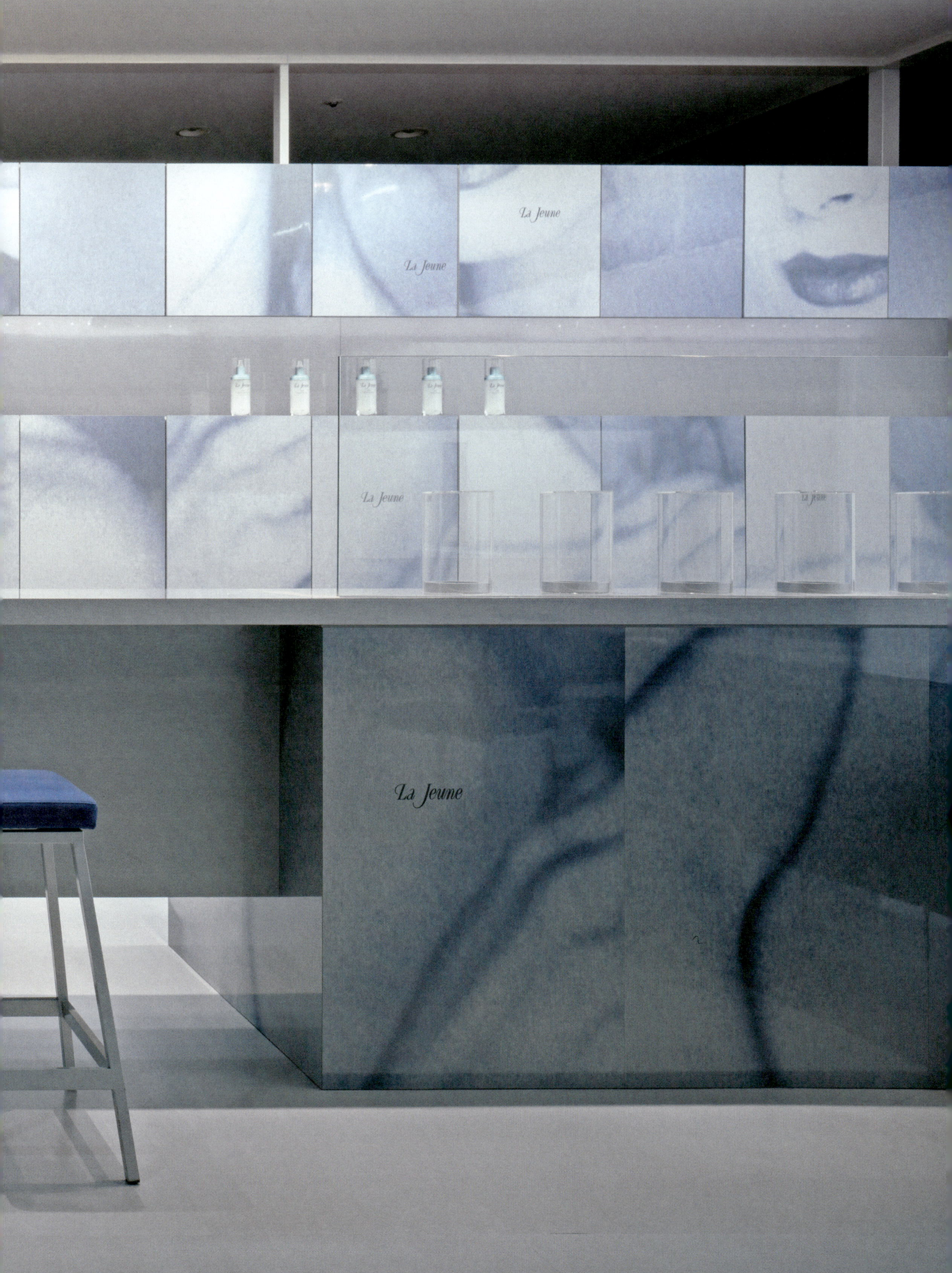
La Jeune
La Jeune
La Jeune
La Jeune

La Jeune

Venus Fort

La Jeune Venus Fort was the first retail location in Tokyo for this anti-aging cosmetics brand. The area allotted for the shop was small, approximately 9-m wide by 2-m deep. Here, I strove towards a spatial design fit not only for providing products, but also for engraving the 'presence of beauty' in people's hearts through the light airiness, comfortable tension and pure transparency of the space.

The first thing I envisioned in the process of my design was the use of aluminum material. As aluminum is a light metal, both physically and visually, I decided it was the perfect material for creating a light impression for the space.

The floor, walls, ceiling, shelves, furniture, counter – as much of the spatial composition as possible – consists of a single material: aluminum. The anodised aluminum boards provided the desired light, airy atmosphere, thereby allowing me to continue on with the project without a single doubt about my choice of material.

The aluminum boards are embossed with convex forms at a 50-mm pitch. The screws used to attach the boards to the wall were positioned based on the convex embossing. In addition, the screws were rounded at the tops to match the convex shapes on the wall. While this project only involved a small amount of space, layer upon layer of experimentation was conducted on the strength of the material and embossing pitch. The display shelf was created from a channel cutting horizontally through the wall. The decision to limit the display space, however, required strong determination in terms of business. Lastly, small chairs with blue backrests and seats were also designed specifically for this shop.

The products sold in the shop prevent aging. Thus, this space was meant to encapsulate the concept of slowing down the process of time. The design was based on a hope that people who spend time here could experience a gentler flow of time than in their daily lives. ×

Where **Tokyo, Japan**
When **August 1999**
Project type **Retail**
Photographer **Satoshi Asakawa**

Wimba Nail College

Wimba Nail College is a beauty school that teaches beauticians about the art of nail design. It is a small facility, attended by only a few dozen people every year. Requirements of the space include classrooms with desks, chairs and a variety of professional equipment.

For me in the design of this space, it was also important to create the necessary *ba* appropriate for learning about beauty and health. This was due largely to the fact that where we are situated greatly influences our creative activities. Such is not achieved through tools or equipment, but through cherishing the factors of the sharp air and comfortable atmosphere of the *ba*. I thus envisioned partitioning the space with glass and effectively incorporating the brand's corporate blue colour. Dazzling light was also used as an accent in the space, with many of the floor surfaces covered with blue-speckled marble tiles.

The meeting room had glass walls incorporated to create an open feel. Glass was also used in the centre partition in the lounge. Looking at space or at objects through glass can evoke a completely different emotion, even if the object itself remains the same. Equipment used by the students can be found displayed on the walls, highlighted with spotlights. Although it is a small space, a fixture similar to a bar counter was established so the space could be used to stimulate communication. This counter itself was covered in the same manmade marble as the floor. ×

Where **Osaka, Japan**
When **December 1996**
Project type **College**
Photographer **Satoshi Asakawa**

Lou Zheng Gang Exhibition

This exhibit was held in the special events hall of a department store – a space which typically is multi-purpose, often used for lively functions like sales events. The question of whether such a space could suffice in presenting Ms Lou's works was thus at the forefront of my mind. There was no end to my worries about how to display these works of historical significance that must be passed down to future generations. The artworks of Lou Zheng to be exhibited included some pieces of over 5 m in length, so immediately I was faced with a challenge: the ceiling was a mere 3-m high. After much deliberation, the overall layout was brought together in a spatial design with a *ki-sho-ten-matsu* story (containing an introduction, development, turn of events and conclusion, as in the four-part layout of Chinese poetry).

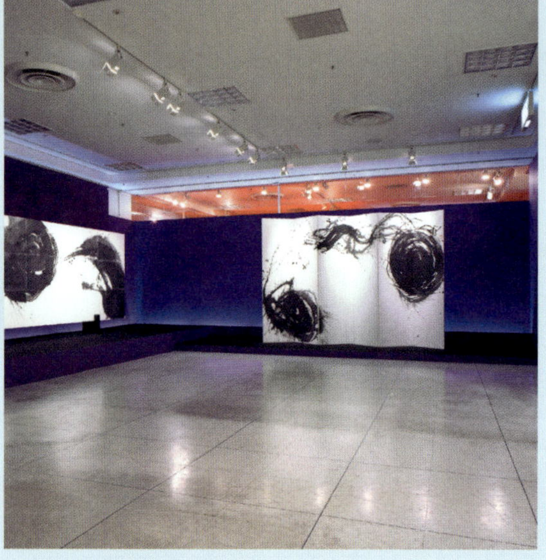

In the *ki* (introduction) space, a large piece on a *byobu* panel called *kokoro* (heart) welcomed visitors upon entering. Huge works over 5-m long were placed in the *sho* (development) space. These pieces, almost twice the height of the ceiling, were exhibited by creating a slope in the space that was neither wall nor floor. This placement, exaggerating the perspective, also further dramatises the dynamism of the pieces.

In the next *ten* (turn of events) space, the sizes of the works became smaller. I created a white space reminiscent of *washi* (Japanese paper), and envisioned the words and the space to meld into one another. The *ketsu* (conclusion) space displayed a compilation of *sho* (calligraphy pieces) created by Ms Lou on a television show. The programme was a talk show inviting many cultured and famous people. This space exhibits the pieces that she sent to all of the people she met on the show. The walls and the floor of the space were covered in a deep red colour called *shoujyouhi*.

The exhibition was created with a specific focus on the viewer. In order for the viewer to sense the full value of the piece, the design was formed based on the perceived distance between the different viewers and the interval and volume between the viewer, the work and the space.

An artist's exhibition is an event for beautifully displaying the works of the artist and providing a pleasant place for visitors to view these works. It is also an opportunity to express the artist's life story through his/her creative activities, including their way of life, ideas and philosophy. As a spatial designer, I feel it is my responsibility not only to interpret the surface value of the work, but to pour all of my efforts into understanding the true nature of the works. It is through this understanding that the works can finally be brought to life. Thus, for the design of this exhibition, rather than an awareness of designing a space, I planned the space as if giving form to a story. ×

Where **Tokyo, Japan**
When **January 2006**
Project type **Exhibition**
Photographer **Kanta Ushio**

'I opted to exaggerate the perspective, further dramatising the dynamism of the pieces'

'I feel it is my responsibility to interpret the true nature of the works'

Nob Dental Office + Nob Kids

It is a well-known fact that the health of your teeth can affect your entire body. The relationship between healthy teeth and beautiful teeth can also be found in the design world. The more functional the design, the more beautiful it will be. The redesign of this space came about because of the relocation of the dental office, which became a good opportunity to realise the ideals of the director in understanding the world from a wider perspective and communicating with society.

What I aimed for here was to create a 'communication space that connects to the city'. A dental office should be a familiar space that can be visited easily. So, the theme for this spatial design was the dissemination of information, whilst creating opportunities for people to learn about healthy lifestyles in order to have healthy teeth. My dental office design not only sought efficient use of space, but also the establishment of hope that could be passed down to future generations.

Here, a contemporary ambience is instilled. The plan was to provide sufficient space in the entrance for a multi-purpose corner, a small gallery-like space normally unexpected in a dental office. It could be used for promoting upcoming events or dental equipment. Various events, developed from a broad understanding of the keyword 'tooth', were held soon after the opening of the dental office. A tooth-brushing corner was installed in a section of the space, for casually receiving instructions about the best way to clean your teeth.

A space was also incorporated exclusively for dental treatments on children. I steered away from incorporating a 'play area' and, instead, considered the needs of both parents and children. My first priority was to create a space where kids could develop an interest in medical matters, making it fun to learn. Also, there were spaces for receiving dental treatment, with private rooms for both parent and child. In addition, the wall material, sofa and shelf design and the mechanisms on the ceiling were all created with a large focus on the keyword 'discovery', to make the space exciting and relaxing for children, and not a place to be frightened of. The first floor counter was planned with the role of a multi-purpose service station for greeting patients, selling products and counseling. Passing through the hallway into the back would lead you to the open and airy examination rooms. This space is charactersed by the distinctive use of colours dispersed across the room. ×

Where **Tokyo, Japan**
When **July 2012**
Project type **Dental Office**
Photographer **Satoshi Asakawa**

DENTAL OFFI
NOB KIDS

'I attempted to create a communication space that connects to the city'

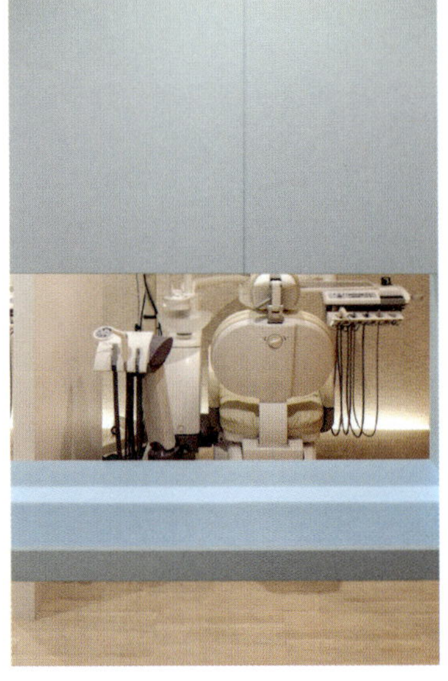

NOB DENTAL OFFICE

NOB KIDS

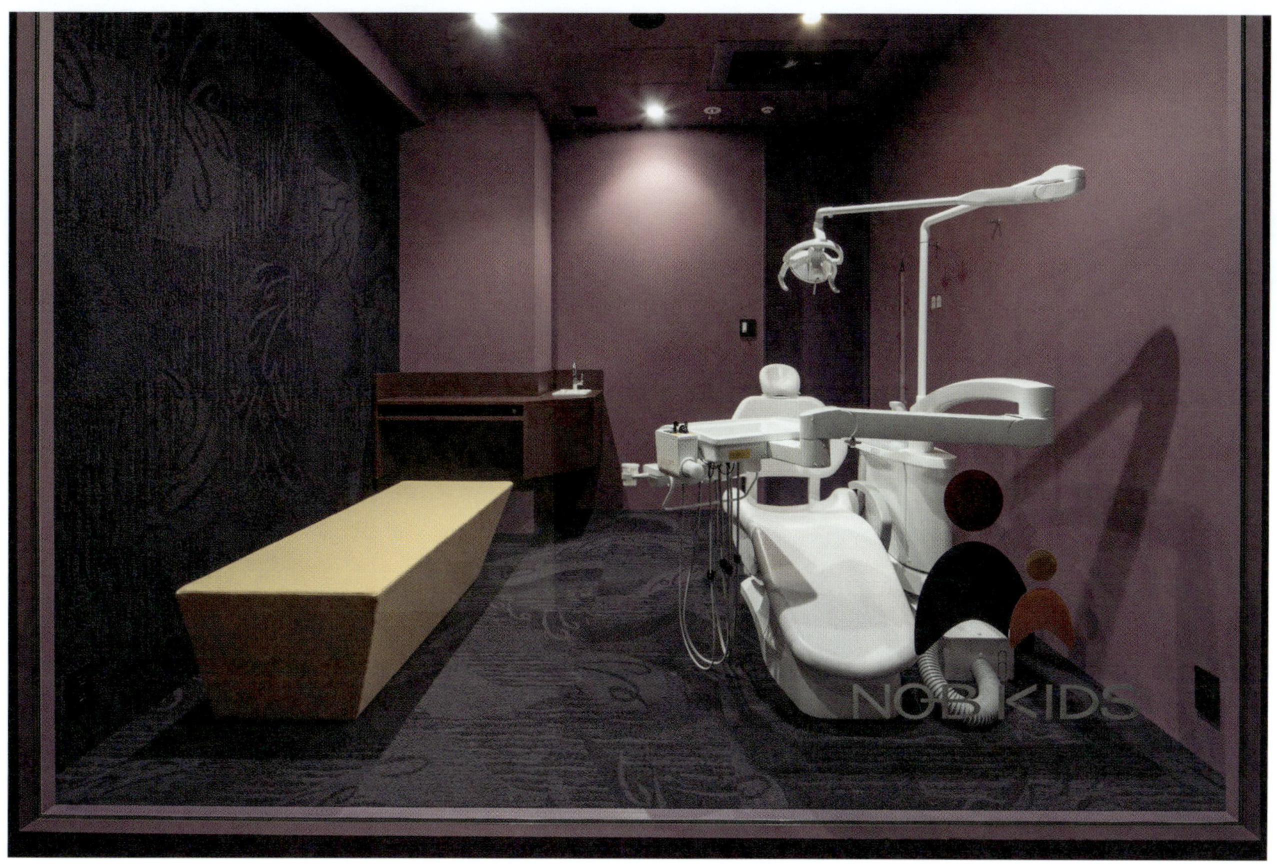

'There was a focus on discovery, making the space exciting and relaxing for children'

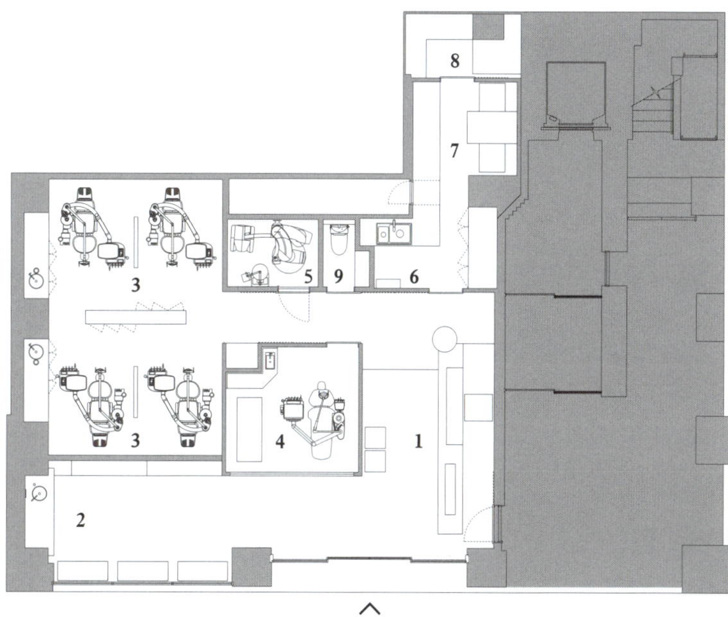

Floor Plan

1. Reception
2. Multi-purpose corner
3. Treatment room
4. Treatment room (kids)
5. X-Ray room
6. Sterilising room
7. Staff room
8. Stockroom
9. Toilet

NOB DENTAL OFFICE

NOB DENTAL
NOB KIDS

Team Tokyo

Following the expansion of Nob Dental Office and the relocation to larger premises, a team of experience staff was established as 'Team Tokyo'. Everyone in this dental practice were able to be allocated their own each examination room due to the a greater amount of space at the new location.

This office takes on a look that is different from the more contemporary design of the Nob Dental Office. With its dark wood and formal decor, here a more corporate ambience is instilled. The sliding partition doors of the waiting room can open up the space to become a multi-purpose room for holding seminars or large meetings. It was my goal to also use this space as a communication tool.

The acoustic design for the project was carried out by Taro Ishida, with a scheme that involved the flow of time throughout the day, starting with a fresh mood in the morning, gradually growing more aggressive during the day and later in the evening becoming a gentle stream of time that envelops the space. In this way, the sound environment was intended to be enjoyable for the staff working in the office as well.

Typically, examination rooms are partitioned such that the maximum number of units are squeezed into the limited amount of space. It is also common to avoid giving ample space to unprofitable areas like the reception or waiting room. This project thus raised an important question towards the modern values of our society in which management of medical facilities prioritise economic efficiency over everything else.

The project may be considered a space in which people review their lifestyles through 'teeth', leading to a reconsideration of healthy living. I am truly looking forward to this development of culture through teeth; in other words, how this new experimental challenge will influence us, not only in the field of dentistry but in creating a new lifestyle.

What this means is that the creation of space does not end once the design is built. The importance of a space comes from the scenes within it; for instance, in a shop, it is the conversation enjoyed while looking at products; in a restaurant, it is the act of conversing while dining; and in these kinds of medical facilities, it is the warm conversations between the doctor and the patient. I cannot help but feel that it is when people gather in a *ba* (place) and various activities begin that the space gradually takes on a life of its own, and the heartbeat of the *ba* can be heard. ×

Where **Tokyo, Japan**
When **July 2012**
Project type **Dental Office**
Photographer **Satoshi Asakawa**

The glass screen and sliding partitions to separate the counselling rooms are fixed in the waiting room.

'It is a space for warm conversations where the heartbeat of *ba* can be heard'

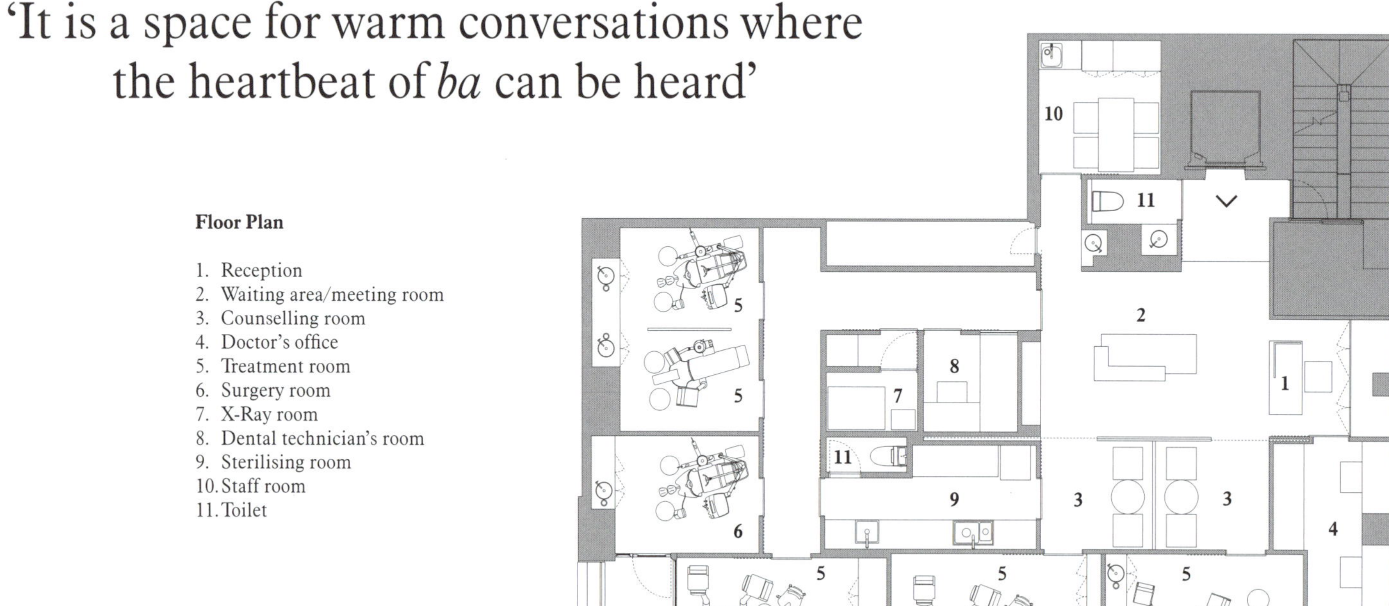

Floor Plan

1. Reception
2. Waiting area/meeting room
3. Counselling room
4. Doctor's office
5. Treatment room
6. Surgery room
7. X-Ray room
8. Dental technician's room
9. Sterilising room
10. Staff room
11. Toilet

Once the glass screen and sliding partition is moved back, space can be used as seminar room for doctors or a meeting room.

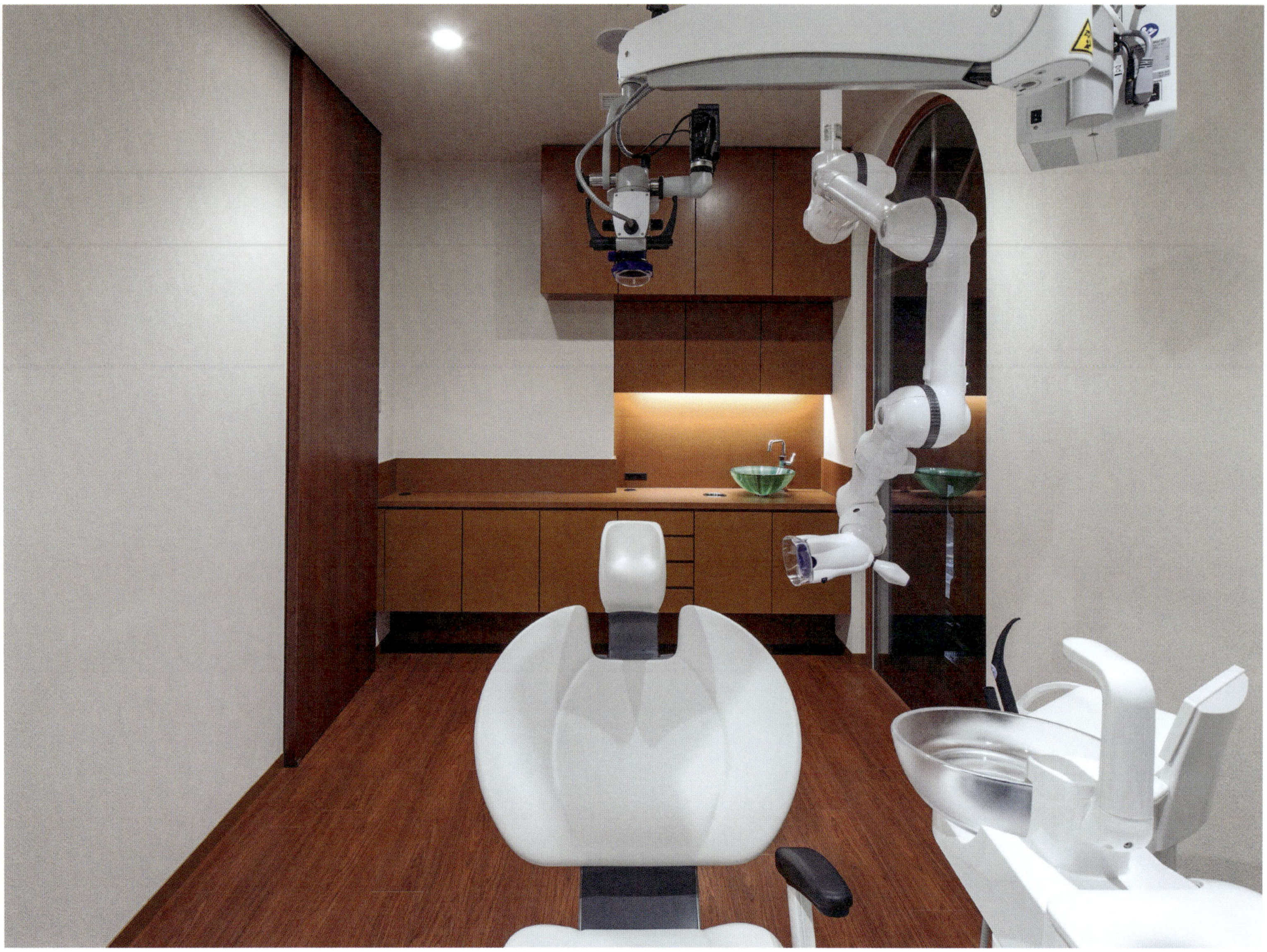

'This project raised an important question towards the modern values of society'

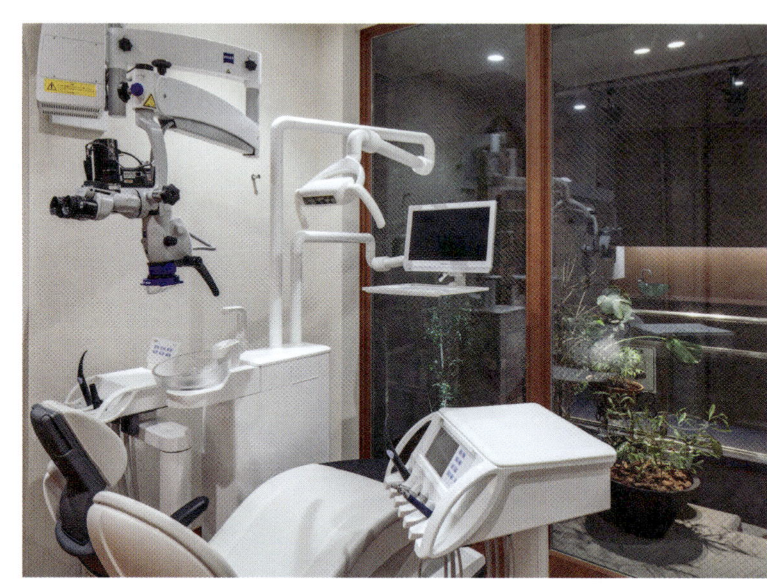

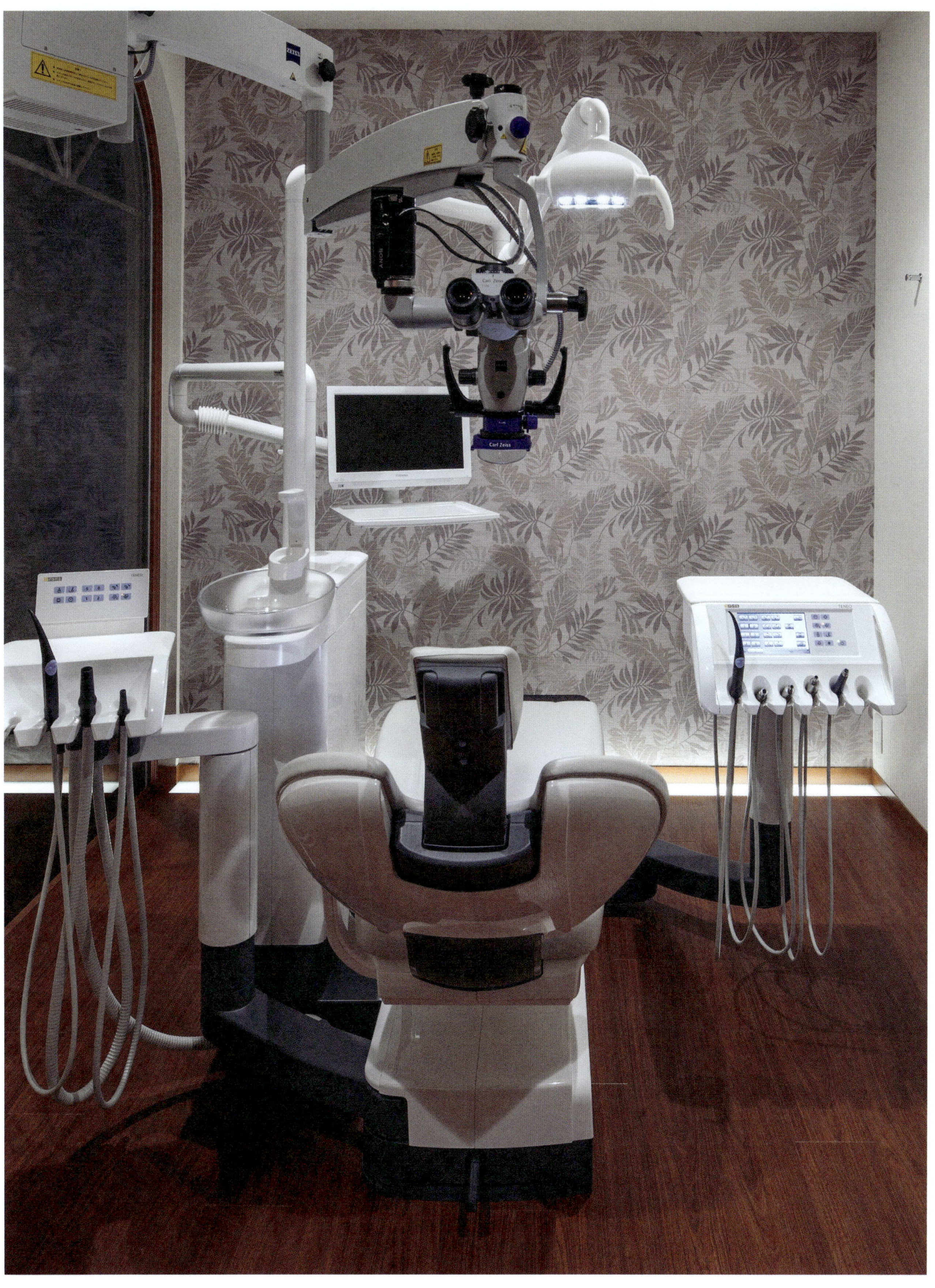
Carl Zeiss

The Tallest and Thinnest

Cold-cathode fluorescent lamps, used behind the scenes in everyday life but not so often as the 'centre stage' light source in lamps, were used here to explore a new light fixture proposal. I imagined that this light source would enable a light fixture with never-before seen proportions. This plan was thus developed using steel pipes 12 mm in diameter, with the vision of designing an ultra-thin floor lamp.

Along with the use of cold-cathode fluorescent lamps, another issue I contemplated was how to switch on the light. My idea was to create a little change in the activities of our everyday lives by proposing a new scene of life in the relationship between light fixtures and people. In most cases, light fixtures are turned on or off with a switch, while others require a string to be pulled.

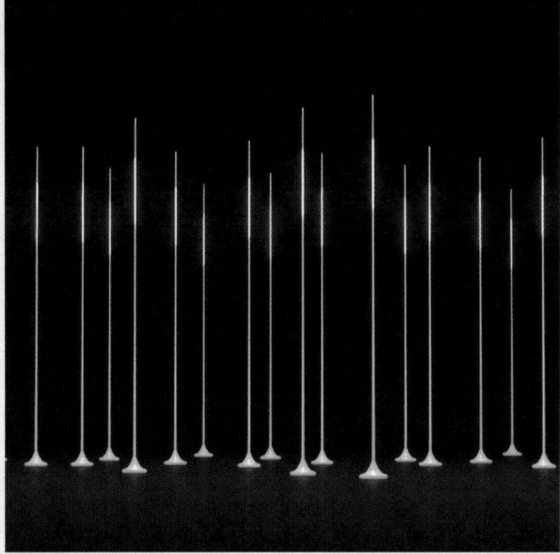

Here, a sensor was built into the 12-mm-diameter steel pipe so that the light would turn on and off when an object, such as one's hand, is sensed within 50 mm of it. While there were countless types of sensors available, it was a challenge to find one that fit in a diameter of only 12 mm.

Although the design took on a simple form, there were many problems that had to be solved before the product could go to the market, such as changing the light or the stability of the sensor system – consequently it was never sold as a product.

I believe that what I am trying to accomplish through the act of creating things with design is something like sowing the small seeds of 'opportunities' for the future. I am not by any means trying to create things that only are sold or that can be sold.

The majority of manufacturers who aim towards commercialisation are likely to hope to create things efficiently or design and develop items that can sell well. It is, without a doubt, only natural for companies to pursue profit. However, as designers, we must face the evils of excessively layered desires for profit and create instead for the future.

I feel an important purpose of design is to contribute to the creation of culture through form. Looking at mankind in the long run, design should support the healthy spirit of the people and gently assist a part of their lives from the aspect of physical form. This role of design in shouldering the happiness of people shall continue to expand further in the future. ×

When **2002**
Project type **Light**
Photographer **Satoshi Asakawa**

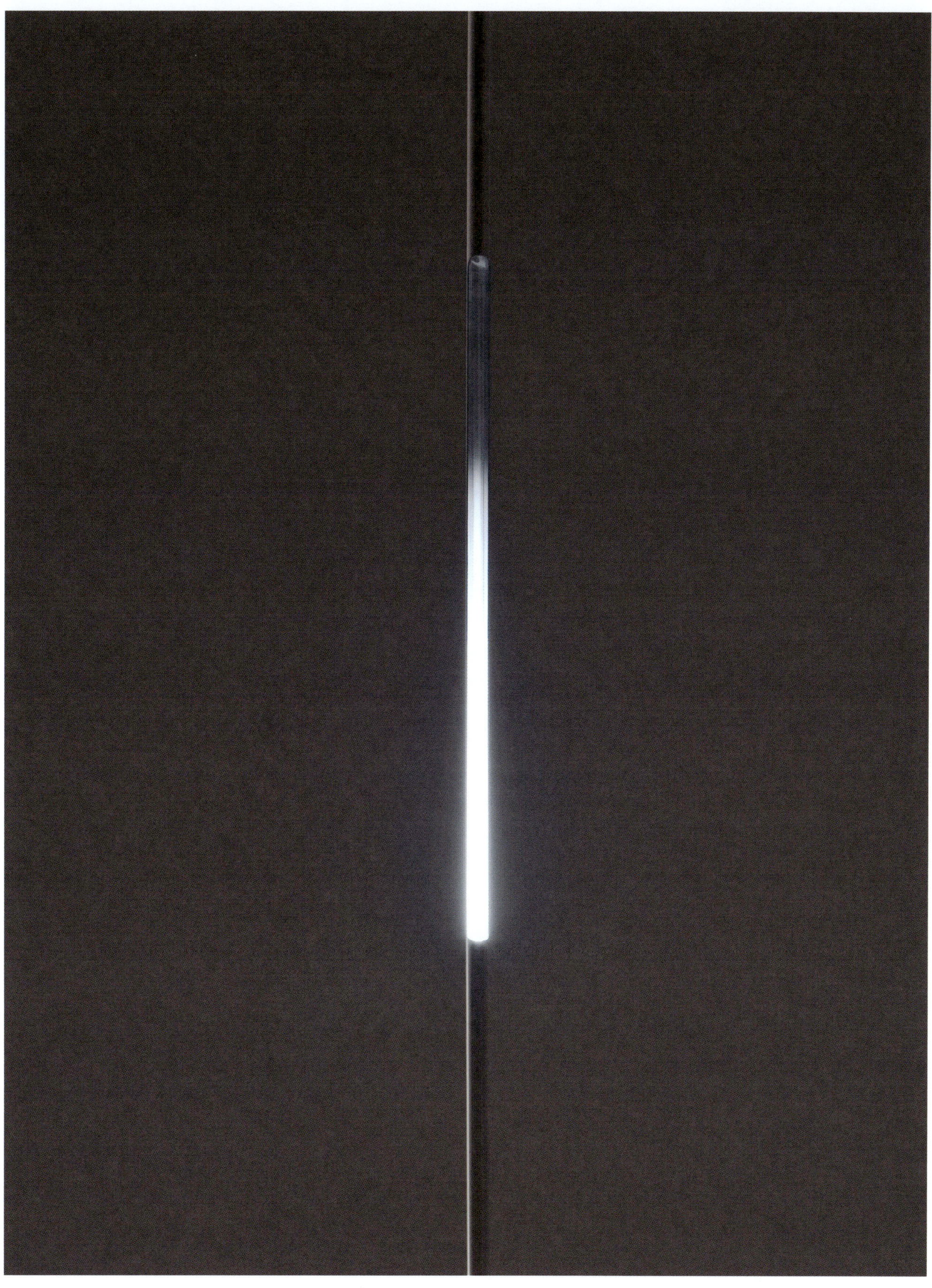

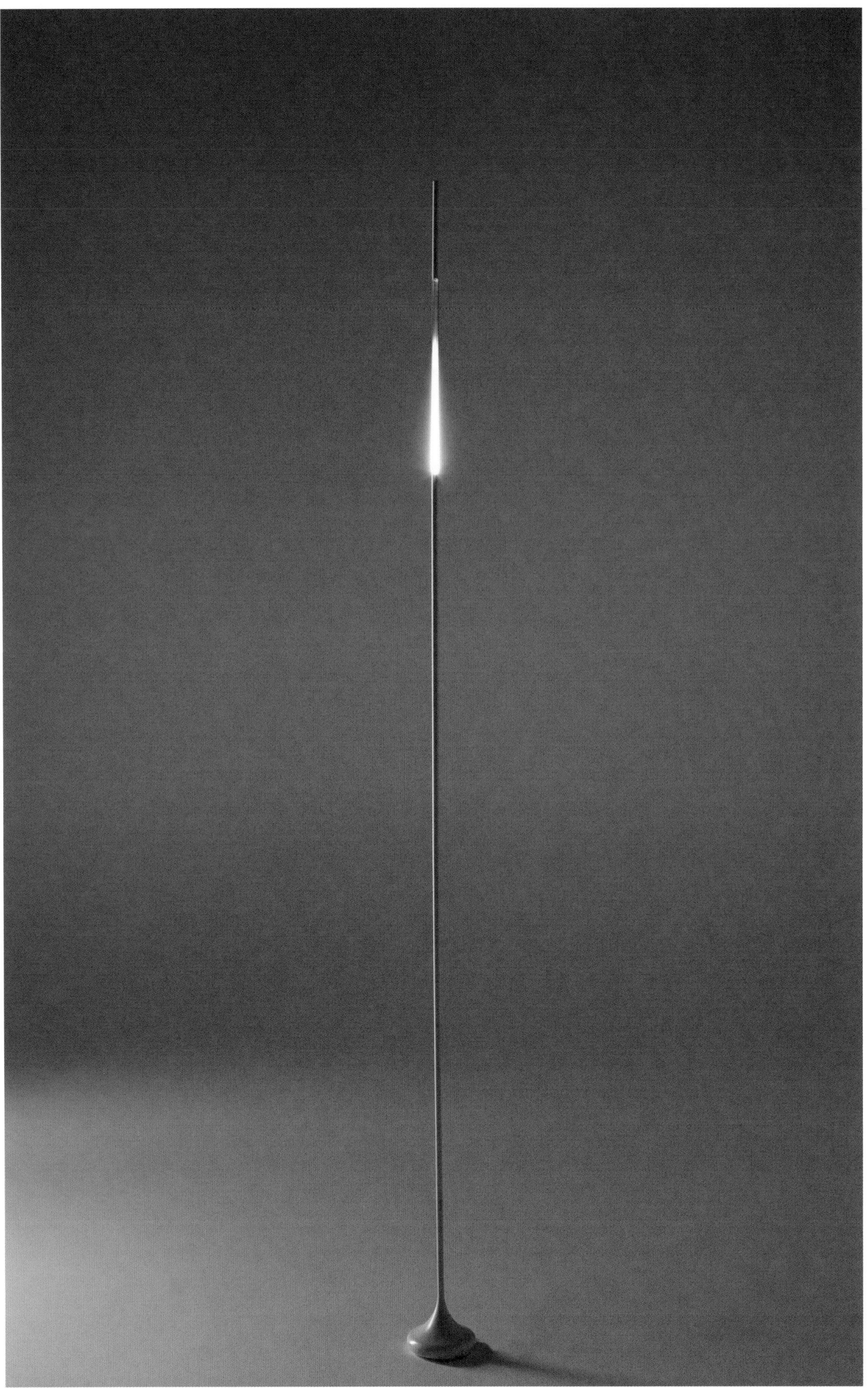

'I feel an important purpose of design is to contribute to the creation of culture through form'

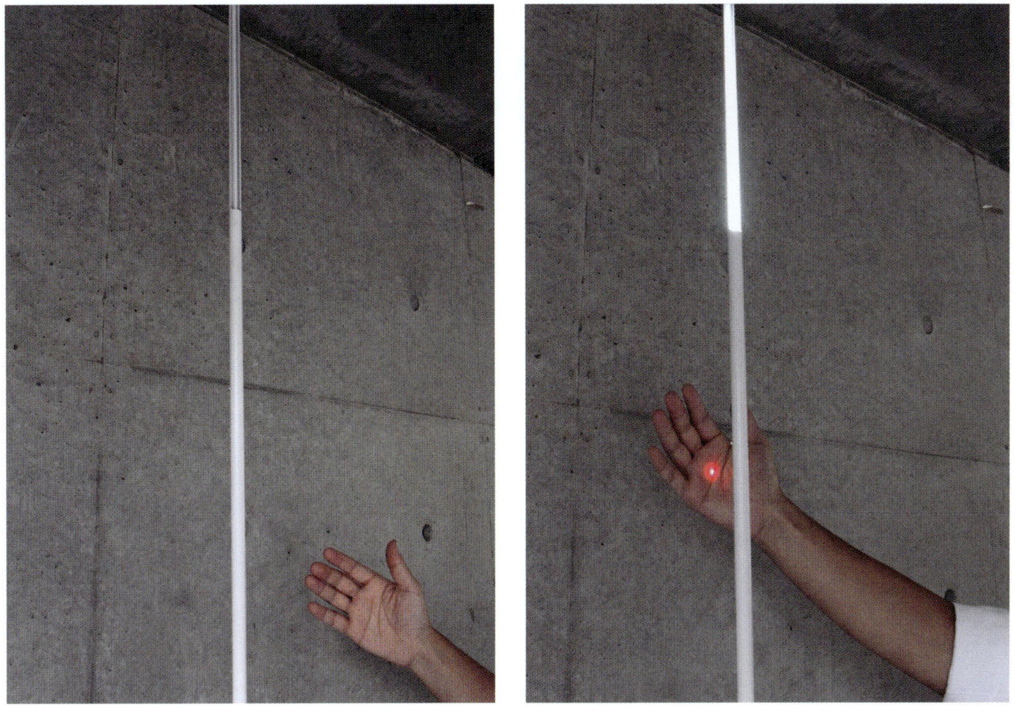

A sensor was built into the 12-mm-diamater of steel.

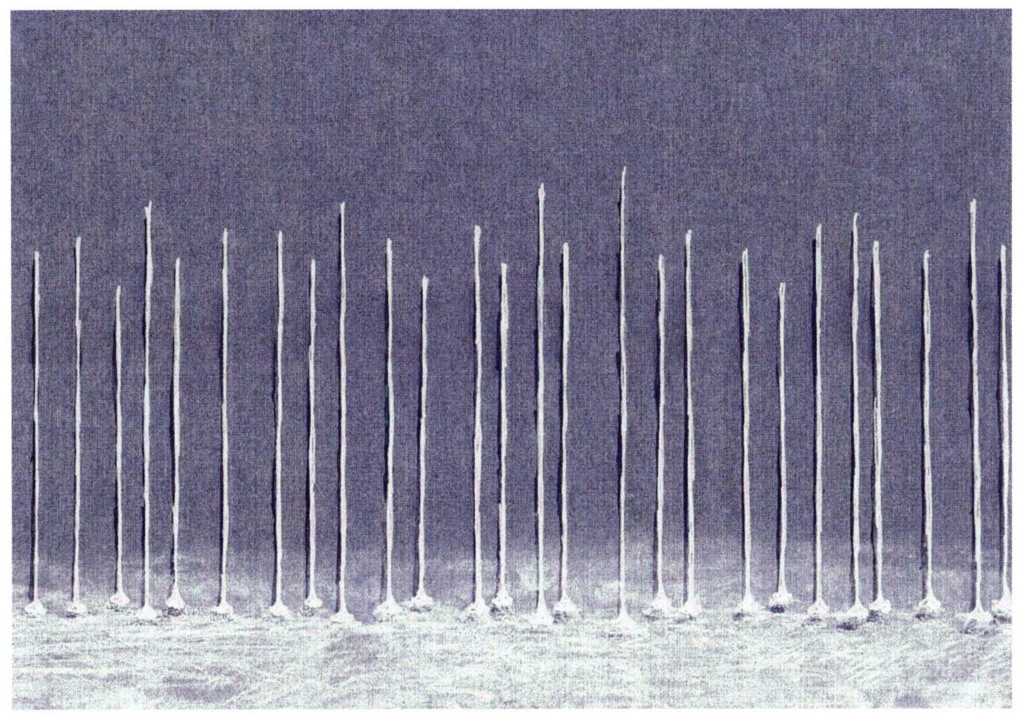

Concept sketch for the 'lighting forest'.

Chieno-Wa

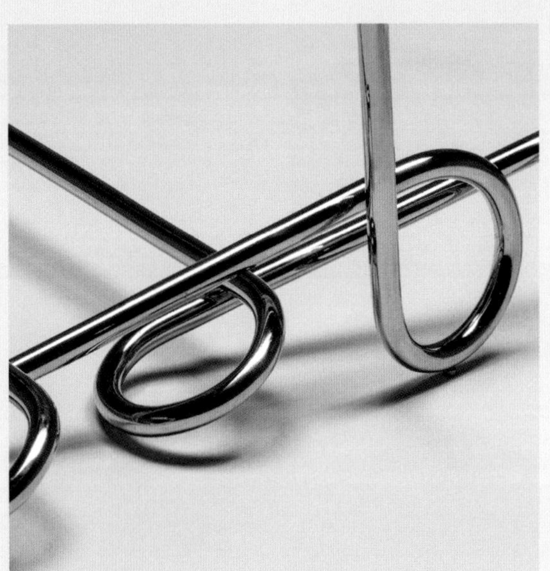

This was a hanger rack that I created for displaying products in my shop designs for Pleats Please Issey Miyake. It is made of a 19-mm-diameter stainless steel pipe, shaped into an independently standing form by bending. As its form was reminiscent of a *chieno-wa* (puzzle ring), it came to be called the Chieno-Wa hanger rack.

Although at first glance, the bending of the rack legs makes it look complex, it can be stacked functionally. If the stacked form is maintained, it is possible to mitigate the fundamental cause of its bulkiness. In order to ensure its stability as a hanger rack when products are hung, solid stainless steel pipes were used on the bottom of the rack.

Initially used only in a number of shops in Japan, the rack has gradually come into use in various countries throughout the world. The design concept was simple, but production itself was far from easy. Production precision appeared in the form of differing balance between the various countries. Overall, I was happy to see that precision clearly increased with repeated production. ×

When **2003**
Project type **Hanger**
Photographer **Satoshi Asakawa**

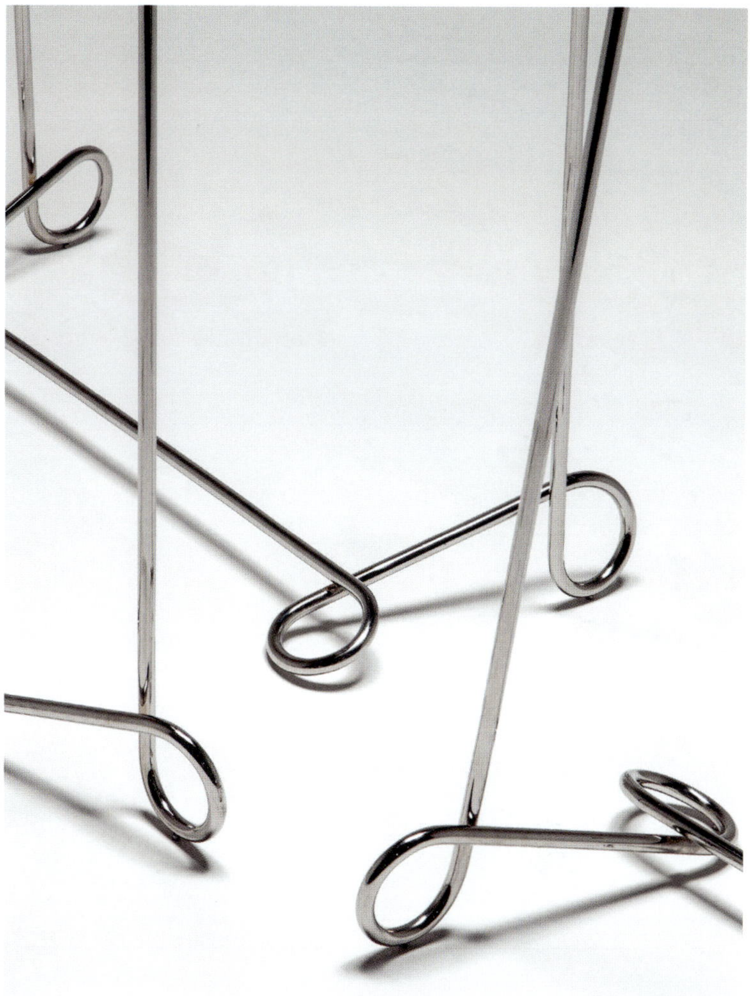

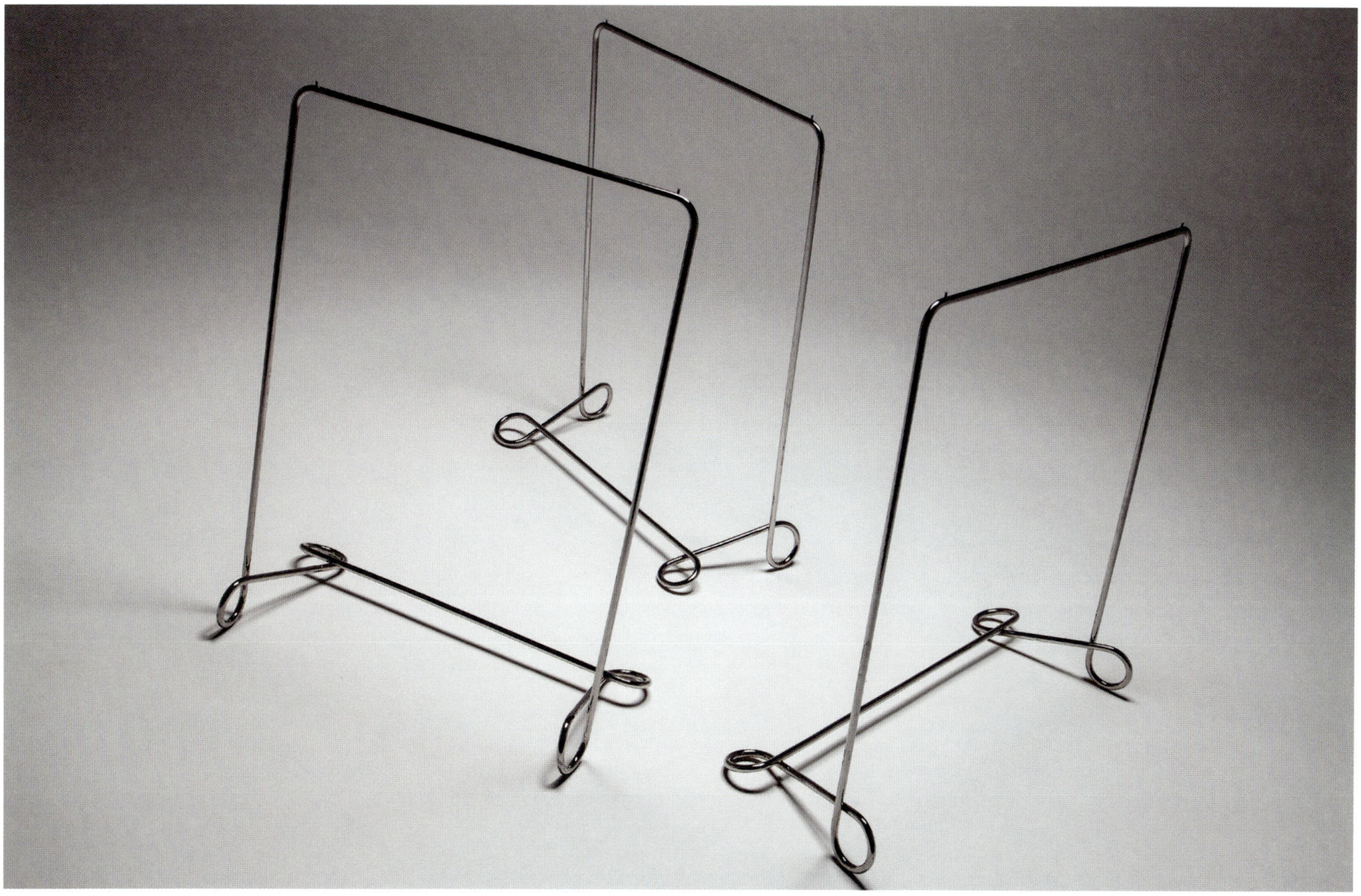

Pipe

Chair, Stand Light, Bench

My Pipe design idea was initially realised in the form of a chair, made by placing stainless pipes 12 mm in diameter side by side. The partially extended pipes draw a gentle curve to form the front and back legs. They further extend upwards to create the backrest. These round pipes with a mirror finish reflect a distorted image of their surrounding environment. The landscape reflected into each pipe appears as a single pattern, and through the succession of these patterns, the chair emits a strong presence that does not meld into the landscape.

This design series also includes an impressive bench. Randomly-placed small arcs form the legs of this bench, with coloured versions also proposed, as well as options for cutting the pipes using Boolean operations. What is common to all these proposals is that they are assembled using only the minimum structural element of pipes. A further developed variation includes a light fixture formed by a chain of pipe rings.

Over time, it became evident that this chair, realised as a case study, had a structural defect of shaking back and forth. Thus, there is still room for improvement with this project, such as increasing the welding area and attaching a tie beam-like apparatus to stop it from shaking. Further studies are ongoing. ×

When **2013**
Project type **Various**
Photographer **Satoshi Asakawa**

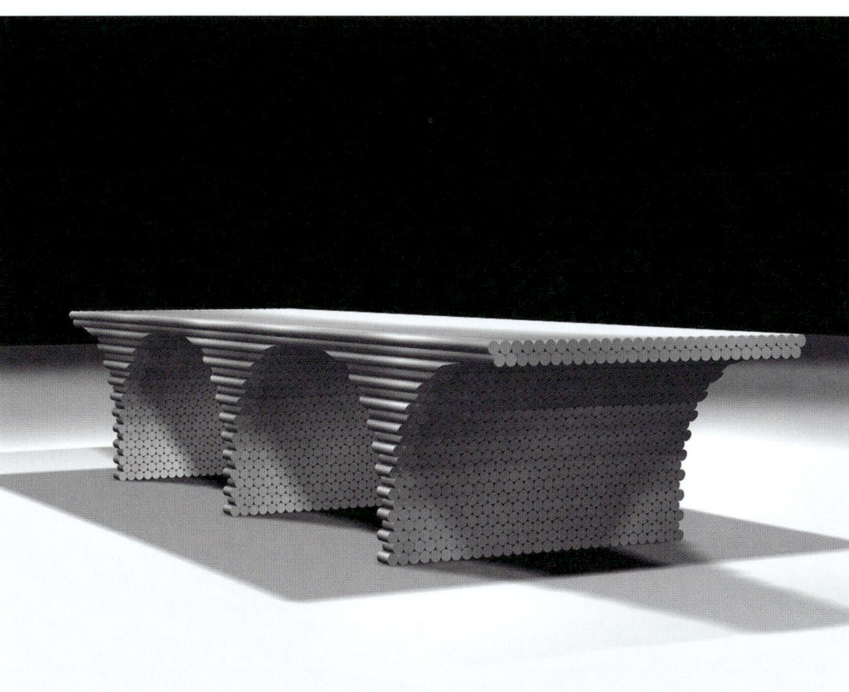

A 3D prototype image of the stand light.

Prototype images of the bench.

Designer Profile

Keisuke Fujiwara was born in 1968 in Tokyo, Japan. After graduating from Musashino Art University, he worked for the renowned Japanese interior designer, Shigeru Uchida. Following an internship at Ron Arad Associates in 2001, he established Keisuke Fujiwara Design Office where he specialises in interior and furniture design. He has participated in international projects and also holds an associate professor position at the Tokyo Metropolitan University. ×

'What I feel in Keisuke Fujiwara's work is a sincere attitude towards design and the outlook of constantly thinking about 'what design is'. The subjects we design for are many and varied. In this case, it makes me constantly think about what 'space' and 'things' we create for, how they should be realised and what their purpose should be. I see this mindset in all the subjects of Keisuke Fujiwara's designs.

The '5 pm in the Summer' project was a new discovery for me when it was presented in 2001. The rich colour of this chair, based on the image of a summer sunset, was made through a process of titanium anodisation. The thicknesses of oxide films gave the piece a variety of light refractions and the resulting colours produced a unique sense of elegance. However, the special characteristic of this chair came more its form than its colour. The high level of attention to the back design of this chair is likely the outcome of Fujiwara's views.

The Spool Chair was made from a Thonet Chair No.14 wrapped in silk thread. This style of chair was produced by Michael Thonet in the 18th century. It was made from bent beech wood and has been loved by countless designers throughout the ages as one of the most symbolic chairs in the world. The fact that Fujiwara took this familiar product and changed it into a new, beautiful and profound chair by wrapping it with silk thread was a kind of discovery to me. The most important thing in design, after all, is the attitude to discover what others have not been aware of.

The Exhibitions of New Textiles Works by Kawashima Textile Manufacturers in 2001 were the realisation of a corporate image. The challenge in this design was to incorporate the tradition of Kawashima Textile Manufacturers and to show the potential of these textiles. A further purpose was

‘What I feel in Keisuke Fujiwara’s work is a sincere attitude towards design and the outlook of constantly thinking about what design is’

Shigeru Uchida

to re-examine lateral ties within the company through these two exhibitions and to create the opportunity for strengthening them. Fujiwara entrusted many such things into the exhibition designs, realising a spatial expression of unparalleled excellence. In the first exhibition, the 500 spools of thread stretched from the high ceiling to the floor below was truly a straightforward expression of Kawashima textiles. The delicate nature of these threads and, further, the countless different colours from red to blue shaped the image of this exhibit.

The shop designs for Pleats Please Issey Miyake in Taiwan and Bangkok, realised between 2004 and 2008, were situated in different locations, but there was a common design challenge between them. Fujiwara divided the space vertically in two, making use of the high ceilings. He created independent images for the upper and lower spaces, creating a light blue space based on the Pleats Please image in order to establish the shop's image in the new locations. The lower aspects became functional spaces that are used for display.

The most remarkable of these shop designs was the one in Bangkok. The high-ceilinged upper space was composed of linear elements that continued on to become hangers and shelves in the lower display area. The walls designed in these stripes functioned as hangers in the lower area. The most outstanding point about this shop was that there was no disconnection in spatial image between the upper and lower areas.

If we are to examine Fujiwara through such works, we must look at the fact that, as designers, we need to constantly think about what design is, who it is for and how it will be realised. This attitude is what you will find in Fujiwara's collection of works.' ×

Shigeru Uchida
Tokyo, Japan

'It was clear at the time that he was a serious designer in the making'

Ron Arad

'We had the pleasure of having Keisuke Fujiwara at our studio for a 3-month period in 2001. He contributed significantly in developing an exhibition that was presented Milan, as well as developing a concept for retail outlets for an Italian telecommunication company. During his time here, his sincere attitude toward design was observed, together with his curiosity and skills. Indeed looking at his independent work that followed, it was clear at the time that he was a serious designer in the making.' ×

Ron Arad
London, United Kingdom

Composing Interior Space

Designing Interior Elements

Keisuke Fujiwara
Interior Elements for Space and Product Design

Publisher
Frame Publishers

Author
Keisuke Fujiwara

Production
Tomohiko Ono (Keisuke Fujiwara Design Office)
Carmel McNamara (Frame Publishers)

Translation
Riyo Namigata

Graphic Design
Mariëlle van Genderen

Prepress
Edward de Nijs

Printing
Ofset Yapimevi

Trade distribution USA and Canada
Consortium Book Sales & Distribution, LLC.
34 Thirteenth Avenue NE, Suite 101
Minneapolis, MN 55413-1007
T +1 612 746 2600
T +1 800 283 3572 (orders)
F +1 612 746 2606

Distribution rest of world
Frame Publishers
Laan der Hesperiden 68
1076 DX Amsterdam
the Netherlands
frameweb.com
distribution@frameweb.com

ISBN 978-94-91727-02-3

© 2014 Frame Publishers, Amsterdam, 2014

All rights reserved. No part of this publication may be reproduced or transmitted in any form or by any means, electronic or mechanical, including photocopy or any storage and retrieval system, without permission in writing from the publisher.

Whilst every effort has been made to ensure accuracy, Frame Publishers does not under any circumstances accept responsibility for errors or omissions. Any mistakes or inaccuracies will be corrected in case of subsequent editions upon notification to the publisher.

The Koninklijke Bibliotheek lists this publication in the Nederlandse Bibliografie: detailed bibliographic information is available on the internet at http://picarta.pica.nl

Printed on acid-free paper produced from chlorine-free pulp. TCF
Printed in Turkey

987654321